DISCOVERIN POLITICS

Edited by David Roberts

AUTHORS

Alan Thompson
Roy Bentley
Shaun Best
David Roberts
Charles Malcolm-Brown
Stephen Wagg
Graham Thomas
Steve Cobb
Jill Longmate
John Benyon
Adrian Beck
David Toke

Causeway Press Limited

INTRODUCTION

Most students now taking 'A' Levels have experienced the new approaches to teaching and learning that accompanied the introduction of GCSE. They are no longer prepared, or required, to be passive learners. They are accustomed to the greater emphasis placed on the type of skills-based, discovery learning which *Discovering Politics* sets out to incorporate and to develop at 'A' Level standard.

This does not make the teacher's role redundant. On the contrary, it requires of the 'A' Level teacher, as well as the student, a wider and more complex range of skills than hitherto. So, although the units in this book can be undertaken with benefit by students working wholly or partly on their own, even greater advantages can come from their use as class or small group exercises employed by teachers in different ways to suit the requirements of their students.

Discovering Politics consists of ten units written by experienced teachers. Each unit takes a particular hypothesis, question or problem which the student tackles by working through a series of activities relating to data from a wide variety of sources including newspaper articles, photographs, diagrams, tables, cartoons, maps and extracts from relevant empirical studies. The data have been selected for their interest and for their potential in stimulating students to attempt the activities. The activities involve linked questions and tasks which encourage the student to interpret evidence, evaluate arguments, critically assess views and draw conclusions. *Discovering Politics* therefore adopts a student-centred, problem-solving approach in which students take an active role in the learning process.

Each unit is self-contained in that all the activities can be tackled without recourse to other texts. Some of the units (such as those on electoral systems, political parties and pressure groups) relate to clearly recognisable topics found in most 'A' Level Politics syllabuses and examinations. Others are concerned with specific issues or themes which cross topic boundaries. The final unit on 'the politics of nuclear power' is a good example of this as party policies, public opinion, the role of pressure groups and the nature of protest are all brought into an examination of the issue. In the volume as a whole, emphasis is given to political representation, participation and behaviour – rather than to political institutions – as these areas have tended to receive less attention in the traditional textbooks.

Earlier drafts of units in this book have been tested with groups of students and have been adapted where necessary. I would welcome further comments from teachers and students on their experiences of using *Discovering Politics*. Please write to me at Causeway Press.

I would like to thank all the authors who have contributed to *Discovering Politics*. They have been prepared to marshal their ideas within the uniform and consistent structure required by a book of this nature. My thanks are due also to Will Wale at Causeway for his work during the final stages of the editing process.

David Roberts
Editor, *Discovering Politics*

Causeway Press Limited
PO Box 13, Ormskirk, Lancs. L39 5HP
© Causeway Press Limited 1989
1st Impression 1989

British Library Cataloguing in Publication Data
Discovering politics.
1. Great Britain. Politics
I. Roberts, David
320.941
ISBN 0–946183–57–0

Typesetting by Chapterhouse, Formby.
Printed and bound by The Alden Press, Oxford.

CONTENTS

ACKNOWLEDGEMENTS

Written and graphical material

The authors and publishers are grateful to all those who permitted the use of copyright material in this book. Due acknowledgement has been made to each source in the text. Items from Social Trends and the Department of Trade and Industry reproduced with the permission of the Controller of Her Majesty's Stationary Office, Crown copyright reserved. Items from the Times, © Times Newspapers Ltd; Daily Mail, Mail Newspapers PLC; The Open University, © 1988 Open University Press. *Social Studies Review* is available only on subscription from Philip Allen Publishers Ltd, Market Place, Deddington, Oxford OX5 4SE (0869 38652).

Photographs and Cartoons

Associated Press p. 10
Atomic Energy Authority p. 103
British Nuclear Fuels PLC p. 52
Central TV p. 40
Department of Health and Social Security p. 55 (top)
Department of Trade and Industry p. 55 (top)
Ingrid Hamer p. 15
John Kent p. 33
Lynton Robins p. 30
Mail Newspapers Ltd p. 42
National Viewers' and Listeners' Association p. 85
Newspaper Publishing PLC pp. 61, 109
New Statesman and Society (Peter Schrank) p. 25
Network – John Sturrock p. 55 (middle), Mike Abrahams p. 98 (bottom right)

Nicholas Garland p. 62, 65
Observer Newspaper p. 54
Pluto Press p. 37
Popperfoto pp. 38, 39 (top), 75, 79, 84, 87, 98 (top and bottom left)
Press Association p. 62
Private Eye p. 40
Prominent Features p. 40
Steve Bell pp. 70, 74, 81
Times Newspapers Ltd p. 11
Trades Union Congress p. 52

Original artwork and cartoons

Ian Traynor pp. 4, 7, 8, 9, 12, 13, 14, 18, 21, 28, 36, 47, 50, 57, 60, 75, 105
Sandy Britton-Finnie p. 69

Cover design

Susan and Andrew Allen

Typing

Ingrid Hamer

Every effort has been made to locate the copyright owners of material included. Any omissions brought to the publisher's notice are regretted and will be credited in subsequent printings.

UNIT 1 From Direct Democracy . . . to Direct Democracy?

To what extent does modern use of the word 'democracy' bear any resemblance to the original meaning of the term?

Introduction
This unit encourages an exploration of this question by comparing the classical definition of democracy with current meanings of the term and by examining some of the features of Western liberal democracies. The latter will involve a consideration of central concepts and characteristics such as **representation**, **majority rule**, **the mandate** and **participation**. Finally, it considers whether modern technology can provide an opportunity of returning closer to those characteristics implied by the original definition of the word.

A. From direct democracy . . .

ACTIVITY 1

After looking at data 1.1–1.3, describe in your own words the essential difference between **direct** and **representative** democracy.

1.1

Ancient Athens

Athens was divided into ten blocks, called *tribes*. Each one of the ten elected 50 men over the age of thirty to a *Council*. Their duty was to carry out the daily work of government. They also made suggestions to be discussed by an *Assembly* of citizens. The Assembly could make laws and decide on peace or war.

Top government jobs were shared out. Judges, Council members and town officials all held office for only a year. Then they were replaced by other men. In this way, everyone had the chance of holding office, whether they were rich or poor. Out of Athens' total male population of about 40,000, therefore, about a fifth were members of Council or officials. At the same time, they were also farmers, shopkeepers and so on, for they had to go on earning their living.

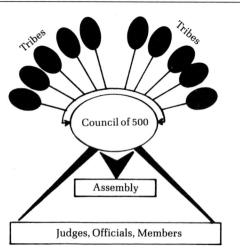

Source: J. Jamieson, *The Ancient Greeks*, Arnold, 1981

1.2

Democracy

The word democracy comes from two Greek words meaning 'people power'. In ancient Greece democracy was the form of government in which all qualified citizens were allowed to participate in the government of their cities. The citizen was expected to play a positive role in government rather than giving the task of ruling to others. This direct form of democracy has been seen as the purest form of democracy. However, even in Greece, large sections of the population – notably slaves, women and children – were not regarded as 'qualified citizens' and therefore were denied participation.

Two distinct views of democracy developed in nineteenth century Britain. With the first view democracy meant people being involved in decision-making and in being able to control their working lives as well as influencing political events. The second view expressed a less direct form of democracy. It was limited to the idea that people should have some say in selecting a government. If direct democracy was impossible in a large industrial society then a representative democracy (in which the people elect representatives to assist in government) was seen as the practical alternative. This second type would mean that most people should be entitled to vote rather than, as with the first view, enabling them to actively participate in government. It is the second view – representative democracy – that has formed the main approach to political thinking in Britain.

Source: David Roberts, *Politics A New Approach*, Causeway, 1986, pp. 6–7
(adapted from A. Renwick & I. Swinburn, *Political Concepts*,
Hutchinson, 1980)

1.3

B. Classifications of democracy

Across the world there are regional variations in the way democracy is defined and classified. In his book *The Real World of Democracy*, C. B. MacPherson refers to three basic forms of democracy: **Western**, **Soviet** and **African**. These are summarized in data 1.4–1.6.

ACTIVITY 2

A For each of the forms of democracy outlined in data 1.4–1.6 provide a brief (one sentence) summary.

B The United Nations has asked you to produce an agreed, global definition of democracy. In a group, decide how you would go about this task.

C Draw up your global definition of democracy.

1.4

Western democracy

During the French Revolution, the idea of exercising democracy through elected representatives and a legislature emerged. This form of indirect democracy, practised in Britain, is frequently referred to as Western Liberal democracy. Closely associated with it is an emphasis on individualism, competition, political rights, equality of opportunity and political opposition.

1.5

Soviet democracy

At the time of Aristotle, many took democracy to mean rule in the interest of the poor. This is used as a justification by Communists that their system is democratic. They argue that Soviet government is rule in the interest of the majority – the working class. In this case emphasis is placed on social and economic rights. Political participation exists but is strictly under the guidance of the Communist Party.

Many argue that this constitutes dictatorship based on the rule of a single party. On the other hand, it could be argued that the Soviet system is closer to the original meaning of democracy as used by the ancient Greeks.

1.6

African democracy

Two views of democracy have emerged in the African context. The first places emphasis on political cooperation where the interest and welfare of the group are seen as more important than those of the individual. Leaders discuss problems until solutions emerge rather than participating in adversarial party politics.

The second interpretation sees 'democracy' as an alternative to colonial or imperial rule. Democracy here is taken to mean self-government; that is, rule by a government composed of people of that country.

C. Representative democracy. Governments and their promises

One of the essential features of Western democracy is the idea that once elected, governments carry out the promises which they make at election time. But do they? You may have heard comments such as 'politicians are all the same; they'll promise anything at election time, but they always break their promises or forget about them once elected'. Is there any truth in such statements?

ACTIVITY 3

Design a method for finding out whether or not governments in Britain have tended to keep the promises they made at election times. Be as specific as you can. Describe your ideas to some other students and ask them to say whether they think they would work and why. You do the same for their plans. Can you come to an agreed method which you all think would be a successful test?

Before the 1970 election The Times attempted to answer the question 'What's a manifesto worth?' with regard to the 1964–70 Labour Government. Lewis Chester carried out the research by looking at the promises made by Labour in their 1964 and 1966 manifestos and comparing them with what actually happened. Some of his results are shown in data 1.7.

ACTIVITY 4

A   Study 1.7. Do you think this is a good method to use to find out whether governments keep their promises? Is it similar to your own? Can you find any problems with this method? Can you correct them?

B   Discuss with a group of students whether you think governments do keep the majority of their promises.

1.7

Lewis Chester's survey

PROMISE	COMMENT	YES	NO
1. Labour will set up a Ministry of Economic Affairs with the duty of formulating, with both sides of industry, a National Plan.	1. A Department of Economic Affairs was set up and produced a National Plan. The DEA was wound up in October 1969.	✓	×
2. Private monopoly in steel will be replaced by public ownership and control.	2. The 1967 Iron & Steel Act nationalised 90% of the country's steel-making capacity.	✓	
3. Labour will give teeth to the Monopolies Commission.	3. Under the Monopolies and Mergers Act, 1965, the Commissions powers were strengthened.	✓	
4. Certainly we shall not permit effective action to be frustrated by the hereditary and non-elective Conservative majority in the House of Lords.	4. The Parliamentary Bill was designed to curb the hereditary principle and reduce the Lords' power to delay legislation. It was abandoned, April 1969.		×
5. Labour will set up a Land Commission.	5. The Land Commission was established in 1967 with the job of imposing a 40% levy on property development values.	✓	

NB Chester examined a total of 37 promises. He found that 19 of them were kept, 13 were not, and five resulted in inconclusive outcomes.

D. Voting . . . for whom?

It is all very well having a vote, but who should we be allowed to vote for? In Britain we elect MPs, European MPs and local councillors. Should we also elect judges and other officials in central and local government? Before attempting Activity 5, study the cartoon and text provided in data 1.8–1.10.

ACTIVITY 5

A Which is the best method of selecting judges in a democracy: secret appointment, openly debated appointment, or election? Give reasons for your answer.

B In a democracy, many people and institutions make decisions on our behalf and claim to represent us. How many of them are elected? Which, if any, do you think should be elected? Give reasons.

C What difference would it make if the unelected people and institutions mentioned in A and B were to be elected? Think about the effect on the people and institutions themselves, as well as the effects on the voters.

1.8

'The President gave me this job because we see eye-to-eye on things that matter. We both enjoy playing golf.'

1.9

State judges

Today almost all states appoint judges to at least some of their courts, most states elect judges to certain courts, and 20 states use a combination of appointments and elections. Elections vary from state to state. In 1982, they ranged from direct popular election (as in Arkansas and Alabama) to election by the legislature (South Carolina and Virginia). Candidates may run on bipartisan tickets (West Virginia and New Mexico) or nonpartisan ones (Michigan and Washington), but judges usually must run as a member of one party or the other. The term of office for most elected judges averages 6 to 10 years; but for some it is 15 (Maryland) and life for others (Rhode Island). In a few states, it is the practice to support the sitting judge when he or she is up for reelection. Massachusetts's judges, except for justices of the peace, are selected by a commission and serve for life, 'conditional upon good behaviour'. In New Jersey, judges are selected by the governor for seven year terms; if they are reappointed, they receive life terms if they demonstrate 'good behaviour'.

Source: Keefe et al, *American Democracy*, Dorsey Press, 1983, pp. 387–8

1.10

Who appoints the judges?

The English judiciary includes few women, even fewer blacks, and nobody under the age of 40. English judges tend to be elderly gentlemen most of whom have had a public school education. A more diverse judiciary is unlikely to be attained while appointment is confined to practising barristers. There are few blacks, women, and Labour Party supporters among the ranks of senior barristers.

Judges are chosen without any public discussion of their identity, let alone of the merits or defects of the candidates. Their appointment receives little, if any, public comment. The reasons why one candidate, rather than another, has been recommended to the Queen remain hidden in the files of the Lord Chancellor's Department or concealed within the breast of those senior judges amongst whom 'soundings' have been taken.

In the USA the President has the power to appoint Supreme Court Justices with the consent of the Senate. A Presidential nominee has to undergo a Senate examination of his record and jurisprudential beliefs. This serves a valuable function in helping to articulate the criteria of a good judge, in publicizing the beliefs of the nominee, in rejecting inadequately qualified candidates, and in focusing public attention on the process of appointment.

The tasks of the President and the Senate are facilitated by the practice of the American Bar Association of assessing whether the nominee is qualified to be a judge.

Source: D. Pannick, *Constitutional Reform*, Vol. 2, No. 3, Autumn 1987

E. Participation or apathy?

The fact that we have the right to vote and to join political parties is one thing, actually exercising those rights is another. Consider the information in data 1.11–1.15.

ACTIVITY 6

A Does the information in data 1.11, 1.14 and 1.15 give any cause for concern about the health of democracy? If so, explain why and suggest how the problems could be tackled. If not, explain why not.

B After referring to the cartoons 1.12 and 1.13, suggest why some politicians might not always in practice favour a higher turnout at elections.

C Are Conservative MEPs right to comment on the British electorate's 'thirst for Euro-knowledge' given the findings of the MORI survey (1.15)? Explain your answer.

D Name some other forms of political participation which may be growing while party membership is declining.

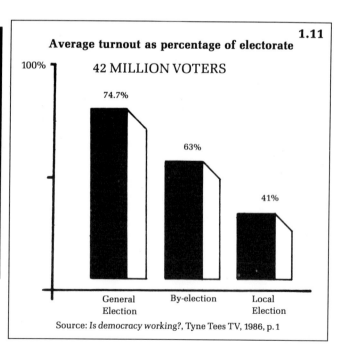

1.11

Average turnout as percentage of electorate

42 MILLION VOTERS

- General Election: 74.7%
- By-election: 63%
- Local Election: 41%

Source: *Is democracy working?*, Tyne Tees TV, 1986, p. 1

1.12

'All you apathetic non-voters stay at home and don't vote, because according to the latest polls I'm going to win.'

1.13

'I like it! It's a blatant appeal to public apathy.'

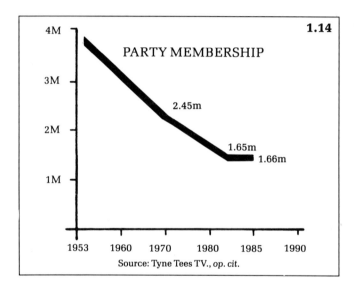

1.14

PARTY MEMBERSHIP

2.45m

1.65m

1.66m

Source: Tyne Tees TV., *op. cit.*

1.15

Uninformed voters 'thirst for Euro-facts'

By James Naughtie, Chief Political Correspondent

The British electorate is largely ignorant of the identity of members of the European Parliament or what they do but nonetheless has "a thirst for Euro-knowledge", Conservative MEPs claimed yesterday.

The poll, conducted in a sample of 2,003 electors by MORI, did reveal some attitudes of a distinctly *communitaire* sort – that a majority favoured a common European passport, for example – but mainly demonstrated the failure of the European Parliament to interest the electorate.

Only 23 per cent of the sample said they were certain to vote in the Euro-election next year (though 18 per cent more said they would be "very likely" to turn out). Of those questioned, 77 per cent did not know when the election was.

Asked to identify the local MEP, 8 per cent gave the correct answer, 5 per cent the wrong answer and 87 per cent said they did not know. Moreover, the respondents did not appear to believe that there was much point in knowing. Asked if anything discussed in the European Parliament had affected them or anyone they knew personally, 78 per cent answered "nothing" . . . 62 per cent of those questioned agreed they would like to know more about the European Parliament.

Source: *Guardian*, 6.1.88

F. Education . . . Who needs it?

Do you need to be well educated before you can really make decisions about how you are going to vote? How often have you heard politicians of opposing parties make seemingly contradictory statements? How are we able to tell which is correct? Can voters still make a valid choice at election times if they are unable to find out 'the facts'?

ACTIVITY 7

A   Look at the two imaginary statements from the politicians in data 1.16. Can you tell which, if either, is true?

B   Now compare the assertions in each statement with 'the facts' (second part of data 1.16). What do you conclude about the accuracy of each claim?

C   What conclusions can you draw about:
   (i)   the need for an educated or informed electorate in a representative democracy;
   (ii) the behaviour of politicians?

1.16

GOVERNMENT

Britain is performing well. The rate of inflation is down by 40%. In the last four years the economy has grown by an average of 3%, half as much again as under the opposition when they were last in power. Our share of world markets is increasing, in 1985 the value of our exports rose by 15%.

OPPOSITION

The government is leading the country to ruin. Inflation has fallen by only 4 percentage points since they came to power, while growth has averaged only 1% a year, only half the average rate achieved by ourselves before this government took over. Our exports have increased by only 1% in volume, even though world trade has been booming. We are losing our share of world markets.

'THE FACTS'

Inflation rate 1979: 10%
Inflation rate 1985:   6%

Growth rate 74–79: 2% per year.
Growth rate 79–85: 1% per year.
Growth rate 81–85: 3% per year.

Exports:
Volume = Physical quantity of goods exported, eg 100,000 cars.
Value = Quantity times the prices the goods were sold at, eg 100,000 cars times £5,000 each = £500,000,000.

G. Majority rule?

An essential element in western notions of democracy is the idea of **majority rule**. The fact that a majority has voted for something is usually seen as justification for it to be carried out. Study the newspaper report in data 1.17.

ACTIVITY 8

A Prepare a brief report to be submitted to the Boundary Commission arguing the case of the residents who have signed the petition referred to in 1.17.

B Prepare a report on behalf of the council to be submitted to the Boundary Commission to refute the residents' case.

C Assuming the residents won their case, what other examples might there be at a **national** level? Debate the issue in relation to Scotland, where at the 1987 General Election the Conservative Party won only 10 of the 72 seats, or Wales, where it won 8 out of 38.

1.17

Suburbs seek split from 'loony' left

RESIDENTS of Britain's most notorious left-wing borough are trying to break free from the "lunacies" of their Labour-controlled council.

More than 10,000 people in Brent, north London, have signed a petition calling for the borough to be split in two.

In the north would be the leafy middle-class suburbs of Wembley, where most people own their own homes. In the south would be Willesden, a typical inner-city area dominated by run-down council housing.

The well-off northerners are tired of the fact that their Tory councillors are constantly outvoted by the hard-left representatives of the southerners

They are upset at a catalogue of Labour decisions which include:

● The suspension of Maureen McGoldrick, head of a Wembley infants school, in July 1986 after she allegedly told a borough official that she did not want any more black teachers there. Disciplinary procedures against her were later dropped on orders from Kenneth Baker, the education secretary.

● Accommodating a homeless Irish family at the luxurious Kensington International Hotel at a cost to the council of £385 a week.

● Ordering posters of households in Brent to include lesbian and homosexual partners.

● Remortgaging the town hall and other public buildings to beat government spending curbs, despite warnings of debts for future generations.

● Hiring 11 personal assistants for committee chairmen, four women's advisers and a nuclear-free zone co-ordinator at a cost of nearly £250,000.

● Disciplining staff who call workmates "dear", "love" or "darling" aimed at eliminating sexual harassment.

The petition, which has been organised by the Brent North Conservative Association, has been sent to the Boundary Commission, which is conducting its first review of London since 1963.

Source: Anne Jacobs, *The Sunday Times*, 27.12.87

H. Representation?

Britain is usually described as a **representative** democracy, meaning that a small number of people are chosen to act on behalf of the population as a whole. The electoral system is the method used for choosing who these people should be. Once they have been chosen, how representative are they?

ACTIVITY 9

A   Explain the cartoon (1.18). What conclusions can we draw from it about the cartoonists view of the Commons as a representative institution?

B   Imagine that the year is 2001. You have been asked to write a report for a new pressure group which claims there needs to be a greater number of male MPs (see data 1.19). What arguments will you use?

C   Do you think that the type of legislation coming from the House of Commons in 2001 will differ from that of the House in 1987? Explain what you think some of the differences might be.

D   Is the House of Commons more or less democratic in 2001 than it was in 1987, or is there no change? Explain your answer.

1.18

1.19

The figures below show aspects of membership of the House of Commons following the 1987 election, and a fictitious breakdown according to the same criteria for a year in the future.

	1987	2001	TOTAL POPULATION 1986 (%)
Total no. of MPs	650	650	
Men	609	27	48.6
Women	41	623	51.3
Blacks & Asians	4	100	4

ACTIVITY 10

A   Explain the possible contradictory pressures on a Member of Parliament expressed in the cartoon (data 1.20).

B   List other possible sources of pressure on MPs.

1.20

ACTIVITY 11

Imagine you are the Member of Parliament in each of the following situations. Make a decision in each case, and prepare the arguments that you will use when you are interviewed by reporters. Ask another student to act as interviewer. In each situation you should explain who you are representing, and how.

A You are strongly opposed to capital punishment. A free vote is due in the House of Commons. National opinion polls show about 70% in favour of re-introducing the death penalty, whilst a poll in your constituency shows 90% support.

B At the General Election, your party's manifesto included a promise to build more nuclear power stations. You strongly supported this proposal. Since your election victory it has been announced that the first of these will be built in your own constituency, close to your rural home. Local opposition has grown quickly and is almost unanimous. Before the vote your Chief Whip reminds you of the manifesto promise.

C You are a male, committed Christian, and strongly believe that all forms of abortion are murder. A Private Member's Bill which seeks to make abortion illegal is to be voted upon. Many women's groups, and the majority of expert medical opinion, argue against the Bill.

I. A mandate to govern . . . Representative versus direct democracy?

In its 1987 election manifesto, the Conservative Party made radical proposals to reform the education system. After their victory, the Secretary of State, Kenneth Baker, published a 39 page 'consultation document', designed to give all interested parties the opportunity to comment on the proposals.

There were complaints from some of the teachers' unions that the time allowed was too short, and that it fell during the summer holidays when few people would be able to meet for discussions. (The document was published in July 1987, with a deadline for submissions set for the end of September, although this was later relaxed after protests.)

The Bill, taking into account the 16,500–20,000 submissions received, was published in November 1987 and became law in 1988.

ACTIVITY 12

A What is a mandate?

B After studying data 1.21–1.23, discuss, in a group, the following:
  (i) why, even though many of the replies to its consultation document were 'critical of the planned reforms, the government made little alteration to its proposals';
  (ii) why Mr. Baker 'refused to publish the submissions';
  (iii) whether the government's mandate to reform education, which it won at a general election, should outweigh public opinion expressed in response to a consultation document, if the two do not agree.

1.21

'If things go wrong, don't blame us. We are only carrying out the people's mandate.'

1.22

Consultation?

Mr Kenneth Baker introduced the Education Reform Bill into the House of Commons last Friday with the claim that it was "a charter for better education". He added, "Its fundamental purpose is to lever up educational standards."

The Bill, which has 147 clauses, will receive its second reading on Monday. Ministers expect that it will complete its committee stage by Easter and have passed through the House of Lords by the summer. They hope to have it on the statute books by autumn of next year.

Despite the unprecedented 16,500 replies received by the Department of Education and Science in response to the consultative documents published earlier this year, many of them critical of the planned reforms, the Government has made little alteration to its proposals.

Only three major changes have been made to the Bill as outlined in earlier documents. The curriculum section has been amended to seem less prescriptive; chief education officers will be required to advise governing bodies on the appointment of heads; local councillors will be eligible for election to the chairmanship of further education colleges.

Source: *Times Education Supplement*, 27.11.87.

1.23

No submission

Julian Haviland, formerly political editor of *The Times* and of Independent Television News, is publishing a book on responses to Mr Baker's consultative documents on the Education Reform Bill.

He is working his way through the 20,000-odd submissions received by the DES which are stored in the House of Commons Library but would appreciate it if organizations who had something to say could send a copy of their submission direct to him.

Mr Baker has refused to publish the submissions and this has angered Mr Haviland. He says it is wrong that such valuable material should be suppressed solely for the convenience of the party in government.

Source: *Times Educational Supplement*, 18.12.87

NB Julian Haviland's book was subsequently published.

J. ...to direct democracy???

ACTIVITY 13

A   Study data 1.24. Although the Conservatives won the 1987 election, some of their proposals did not command the support of a majority of those responding to opinion poll questions. However, it is still accepted that the Government has a mandate to carry out all of its election pledges. Is this fair? Explain your answer.

B   Study data 1.25–1.26. Would you like to see 'ballots on "direct democracy" propositions' used in this country? Give reasons for your answer.

1.24

Public Opinion

PROPOSAL	% FOR	% AGAINST
Privatise British Airports Authority	43	43
Replace Polaris with Trident	31	33
Schools to opt-out	35	45
Privatise Electricity	34	56
Privatise Water	30	59

Source: *Mori*

1.25

"So far, my mail is running three to one in favor of my position."

1.26

Ballots on 'Direct Democracy' Propositions

An increasingly important aspect of US elections are the propositions which are included on the ballot papers in various states. There were some 226 propositions put forward in November 1986, and these included the banning of state-funded abortions (defeated in Rhode Island, Oregon and Massachusetts, but passed in Arkansas), the abolition of property taxes in Montana (defeated), the mandatory wearing of seatbelts in Nebraska (passed), a compulsory decontamination of toxic-waste sites in New York and Massachusetts (passed) and legalisation of growing and possessing marijuana in Oregon (defeated).

A number of important propositions were on the ballot paper in California. Proposition 64, supported by the controversial politician Lyndon LaRouche, would have imposed compulsory isolation on AIDS sufferers; it was defeated. A contentious proposal that was approved makes English the official language of California. This initiative was strongly opposed by various groups, on the grounds that it is racist and discriminatory, and the decision is likely to be challenged in US courts. California also voted heavily in favour of anti-pollution measures; although strongly opposed by business and industrial interests, the support of Jane Fonda, her husband state senator Tom Hayden, and other personalities such as Barbra Streisand, ensured success for the environmentalists' campaign. Also in California, the State's first-ever woman Chief Justice was defeated after nine years in office. Miss Rose Bird consistently refused to impose the death penalty, and a concerted campaign by supporters of capital punishment culminated in a large majority against her.

Source: John Benyon, 'USA Election Report', *Social Studies Review*, Vol. 2 No. 4

Computers and information technology are increasingly affecting people's daily lives. Data 1.27 and 1.28 give examples. Is it possible that new computer technology could be used to make democracy in this country more *direct*?

ACTIVITY 14

A Work out some proposals for using new technology in the democratic system.
B Who would benefit from the introduction of your proposals?
C Who would suffer?
D What changes in the impact of new technology on democracy in the UK do you think are likely over the next 25 years?

1.27

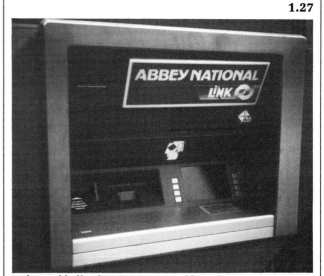

In the world of banking it is now possible to obtain cash, deposit money, order statements, by using a personalised plastic card in a 24-hour machine in the High Street.

1.28

TSB Speedlink

Speedlink is TSB's telephone banking service.

Speedlink gives you direct access to your account round the clock, around the world, simply and conveniently by using the phone.

Gone is the need to visit your branch every time you wish to make a transaction or ascertain your balance. Gone is the need to use envelopes and stamps to pay your bills or to queue in a number of places to transact your business.

Using TSB Speedlink you can:

– Obtain an up-to-the-minute balance of your accounts.
– Transfer money between your accounts.
– Pay your household bills.
– Enquire about the last six transactions on your account.
– Enquire on a particular transaction.
– Request a statement to be sent by post, or uniquely, to a Fax machine.

Further reading

Dearlove, J. & Saunders, P., *Introduction to British Government*, Polity Press, Oxford, 1984

Lynn, J. & Jay, A., *Yes Minister* Vols. 1, 2 & 3; *Yes Prime Minister* Vols. 1 & 2, BBC Publications, London; 1981, 1982, 1983, 1986, 1987

Ponting, C., *Whitehall, Tragedy and Farce*, Hamish Hamilton, London, 1986

Renwick, A. & Swinburn, I., *Basic Political Concepts*, Hutchinson, London, 1980

Wilson, D. (ed.), *The Secrets File: The Case for Freedom of Information in Britain*, Heinemann, London, 1984

UNIT 2 Electoral Reform

'... If you want a great issue, absolutely on a par with the Great Reform Act, the Emancipation of Women, I give it to you:

Fair voting, Proportional Representation

Fair voting in Parliament, in local council chambers, in the European Parliament so that they can genuinely represent the view of the people.'

(David Owen, *speech to the SDP conference in Torquay, 1988*)

Introduction
In working through this unit you will be examining the case for reform of the electoral system in the United Kingdom. Alternative systems and the experience of other states are considered. The problems of bringing about reform are also taken into account. This examination will enable you to assess the opinion expressed above by David Owen, leader of the SDP.

A. How representative is the 'first past the post' system?

The system used for parliamentary elections in the United Kingdom is known as **'first past the post'** or **simple majority**. Each elector has one vote. Each constituency has one Member of Parliament. The candidate with the most votes wins whether or not he or she has an overall majority of the votes cast. The system can be illustrated by considering the result of the Oxford East constituency in the 1987 General Election (data 2.1).

ACTIVITY 1
A Who won the seat? (2.2)
B What percentage of the voters voted against the winning candidate?
C What percentage of the electorate voted for the winning candidate?
D Using the data in table 2.2 and the information in 2.1, do you think that Andrew Smith, the Labour Member of Parliament for Oxford East, can claim to speak on behalf of the voters in his constituency?

2.1
ANDREW SMITH

ANDREW SMITH is 36. Home is in Oxford, with his wife Val and son Luke. He has lived in Oxford for 18 years. Andrew studied at Oxford University and works as Education Officer for the Oxford and Swindon Co-op.

As a City Councillor Andrew spearheaded the drive for better leisure – new playgrounds, help for sports and for children's summer playschemes, and the new Temple Cowley swimming pool. He led the way on improvements to the environment and planning for local jobs and homes.

Andrew Smith has helped many local people. He works closely with residents groups – and with the community relations council – to solve local problems. Andrew is a member of Oxfordshire Age Concern and helped to set up Oxford's new Pensioners' Forum. He is president of a local youth football club.

Andrew Smith understands the needs of our schools and colleges at first hand – through his service as a Governor of two local schools and of Oxford Polytechnic.

Many of you know Andrew through his excellent record of work on local issues like Austin Rover and the Health Service.

Andrew is part of the local community. He is always ready to listen. He has served Oxford East with ability and success.

Source: *Labour Party Election Leaflet*, Oxford East Constituency, 1987

2.2
Oxford East General Election result, 1987

Electorate 62,125

PARTY	CANDIDATE	VOTES	% OF VOTES
Labour	A. Smith	21,103	43.0
Conservative	S. Norris	19,815	40.4
Alliance	M. Godden	7,648	15.6
Green	D. Dalton	441	0.9
Community	P. Mylvaganam	60	0.1

Turnout 79%

Source: *The Guardian*, 13.6.87

In a general election in the United Kingdom there are 650 parliamentary seats contested. The general election is called by the Prime Minister, though the Monarch has to give consent. General elections must take place at least every five years but a Parliament may be dissolved by the Queen, acting on the Prime Minister's advice, before the end of the full legal term. The results for the 1987 General Election are given in data 2.3.

ACTIVITY 2
Study data 2.3.

A Which party won the election?
B What percentage of the votes did it receive?
C What percentage of the voters voted against the party that won?
D The Conservative Government led by Mrs Thatcher claimed that it had a mandate to govern the country. What is your view of this claim?

2.3

1987 General Election – Summary of voting

PARTY	VOTES	% SHARE OF VOTES	CANDIDATES	MPs ELECTED
Speaker	24,188	0.1	1	1
Conservative	13,736,337	42.2	632	375
Labour	10,029,944	30.8	633	229
Liberal	4,173,354	12.8	327	17
SDP	3,167,798	9.7	306	5
Scottish National	416,873	1.3	71	3
Plaid Cymru	123,589	0.4	38	3
Green	89,753	0.3	133	—
Northern Ireland parties	730,152	2.2	77	17
Other	37,576	0.1	106	—
Total	32,529,564	100.0	2,324	650

Source: *Fact sheet 47*, Public Information Office, House of Commons

The 'first past the post' system of voting means that the number of seats that a party wins is not proportionate to the total of votes cast. The pie charts (data 2.4) illustrate this by portraying the share of the votes cast in 1987 and the relative shares of the seats won by the main parties.

ACTIVITY 3
Study data 2.4.

A Distinguish between parties that are under-represented and those that are over-represented in the House of Commons compared with votes cast.
B Which parties would you expect to favour electoral reform and which ones favour maintaining the present system?

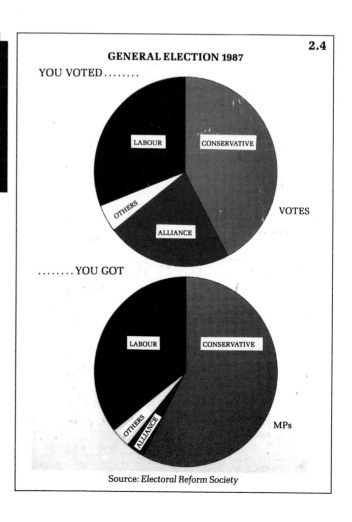

2.4

GENERAL ELECTION 1987

YOU VOTED........

........YOU GOT

Source: *Electoral Reform Society*

The 1987 General Election was not untypical of recent general elections. The 1979 and 1983 results also produced Conservative Governments with substantial parliamentary majorities yet with only a minority of the popular vote.

ACTIVITY 4

Study the extract from Iain McLean's article (2.5)

A   Which party may feel most aggrieved by the lack of 'proportionality' in the election results?

B   What do you think Iain McLean means when he says 'electoral reform remains on the intellectual, if not . . . the political, agenda'?

2.5

The 1987 election result ensures that electoral reform remains on the intellectual, if not necessarily the political, agenda in the United Kingdom. Once again, the relationship between votes cast and seats won for each party was eccentric, as Table 1 shows.

Table 1
Proportionality of seats to votes: UK Parliaments 1979–87

	1979		1983		1987	
	Votes %	Seats %	Votes %	Seats %	Votes %	Seats %
Conservative	43.9	53.4	42.2	61.1	42.0	58.3
Labour	36.9	42.4	27.6	32.2	30.7	34.8
Liberal (/SDP)	13.8	1.7	25.4	3.5	22.4	3.4
Plaid Cymru	0.4	0.3	0.4	0.5		
SNP	1.6	0.3	1.1	0.3	1.4	0.5
NI unionist	1.3	1.7	1.4	2.3	1.6	2.0
NI nationalist	0.6	0.2	0.9	0.3	1.0	0.6
Other	1.5	0.0	1.0	0.0	0.5	0.0
Total	100	100	100	100	100	100
Proportional index (to nearest integer)		85		76		79

Note: 1987 figures are provisional. The proportionality index is the sum of the difference between each party's seat share and its vote share, all divided by 2 and subtracted from 100.

On Richard Rose's index of proportionality, the UK since 1983 has had the least proportional Parliament in the democratic world. Where a score of 100 means a perfect relationship between parties' share of the vote and of seats, a score of 50 means no association, and a score of 0 means that parties which get no votes get all the seats, the 1983 Parliament scored 76 and the 1987 one scored 79.

Source: 'Ships that pass in the night: electoral reform and social choice theory', Iain McLean, *The Political Quarterly* Vol. 59, No. 1, Jan/March 1988

The electoral system has remained essentially the same this century. Since the Second World War the system has tended to produce governments with majorities in the House of Commons. Yet from 1918 until 1945 coalition/minority governments were more common.

ACTIVITY 5

A   What do the terms 'coalition' and 'minority government' mean?

B   Look at how this data has been represented visually in data 2.6. For how many years since 1945 have there been minority governments?

C   How could this trend be used to help argue the case for electoral reform?

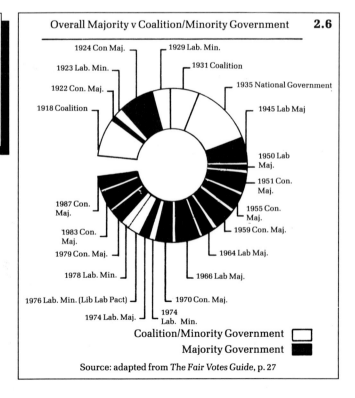

Overall Majority v Coalition/Minority Government   **2.6**

1924 Con Maj.
1929 Lab. Min.
1923 Lab. Min.
1931 Coalition
1922 Con. Maj.
1935 National Government
1918 Coalition
1945 Lab Maj
1950 Lab Maj.
1951 Con. Maj.
1987 Con. Maj.
1955 Con. Maj.
1983 Con. Maj.
1959 Con. Maj.
1979 Con. Maj.
1964 Lab Maj.
1978 Lab. Min.
1966 Lab Maj.
1976 Lab. Min. (Lib Lab Pact)
1970 Con. Maj.
1974 Lab. Maj.
1974 Lab. Min.

☐ Coalition/Minority Government
■ Majority Government

Source: adapted from *The Fair Votes Guide*, p. 27

In February 1974 a minority Labour Government was formed when Labour gained the largest number of seats in the House of Commons. However, they lacked an overall majority; that is, enough seats to outvote all the other parties put together. Another general election was held in October 1974 when Labour gained a small overall majority. This was lost later in a series of by-election defeats so the Lib/Lab pact was formed. The Liberals agreed to support Labour in office in return for consultation. The pact broke down in 1978 and Labour lost a vote of confidence in the House of Commons in 1979. The Conservatives won the ensuing election and two subsequent general elections.

ACTIVITY 6

A Why should a government consider it important to have an *overall* majority in the House of Commons?

B What do you think should be the principal function of an electoral system: to elect a government or to produce a proportionately elected chamber? Give reasons for your answer.

B. Examining other systems

The United Kingdom is relatively unusual in using the 'first past the post' system. Many other methods of voting exist and some countries use more than one. A Royal Commission, appointed to inquire into electoral systems in 1910, claimed that there were over 300 either actually in existence or potentially available. The purpose of this section is to outline the alternatives.

Majoritarian systems. With these the winning candidate must have gained more than 50% of the vote. The two methods generally used are the **alternative vote** and **second ballot**.

ACTIVITY 7

A After studying data 2.7 and 2.8 organize an election in your class using the 'first past the post' system and then the alternative vote. Compare the results.

B Look back to the Oxford East election result (2.1). Imagine that the ballot was conducted under an alternative vote system and that the second preferences of the Alliance voters split two-thirds in favour of the Conservative and one-third in favour of the Labout candidate. Who would have won?

2.7

The Alternative Vote

One option is the Alternative Vote, which is used in the Australian House of Representatives and retains single-member constituencies like the present ones. Rather than placing a mark against a single name, each voter numbers the candidates listed on the ballot paper in order of preference (eg 1st: Labour; 2nd: Liberal; 3rd: Conservative).

If any candidate achieves an overall majority right away (ie more than half the first preferences of voters on the first count), then he or she is elected. If not, the candidate with the lowest number of first votes is eliminated and the second preferences of voters for him or her are allocated to the other candidates as indicated. This process is repeated through later counts, with bottom candidates falling out at each stage and their votes allocated to those remaining until one of these achieves an overall majority.

There is no obligation upon voters to indicate any specific number of preferences. In 'safe' seats dominated by one party, it is likely that the supporters of that party at least would vote for it and express no later preferences. In marginal seats it is more likely that voters would express their second or third preferences (though again they need not do so): in this way, even if they could not secure the victory of the party they strongly supported, they could try to block the one they most strongly opposed.

Source: Peter Hain, *Proportional Misrepresentation*, Wildwood House, 1986, p. 91

2.8

A ballot paper for an alternative vote system

Form F

(To be initialled on back by Presiding Officer before issue)

BALLOT PAPER

COMMONWEALTH OF AUSTRALIA
STATE OF TASMANIA

Electoral Division of DENISON

Election of One Member of the House of Representatives

Directions.—Mark your vote on this ballot-paper by placing the numbers 1, 2, 3 and 4 in the squares respectively opposite the names of the candidates so as to indicate the order of your preference for them.

CANDIDATES

☐ **COATES, John**

☐ **HAY, John Charles**

☐ **HODGMAN, Michael**

☐ **STANTON, Cathryn Marie**

Source: V. Bogdanor, *What is Proportional Representation?* 1984

The **second ballot** operates on a similar principle to the alternative vote. A successful candidate must win a majority of the votes cast on the first ballot. If not, a second ballot is held with the minority parties dropping out leaving only two candidates in the contest. This ensures that the winner has more than 50% of the vote. Until 1986 this was the system that the **French** used for the elections to the National Assembly (2.9).

ACTIVITY 8

A What is the main difference between the second ballot and the alternative vote?
B What advantage might there be with the second ballot?
C Study data 2.9. What might be the disadvantages of this system?

2.9

Example of France

In France, in the National Assembly elections of 1981, the parties of the non-Communist left – primarily the socialists – secured an absolute majority of the seats for only 38 per cent of the popular vote on the first ballot:

	% votes	% seats
Communists	16	9
Non-Communist left	38	62
Gaullists	21	15
Non-Gaullist right	22	14

Source: V. Bogdanor, Op. Cit

Proportional systems. Proportional representation in Parliament could be achieved by one of two different methods; either the **single transferable vote** or the **list system**. Each has a number of variations. The single transferable vote is advocated by most supporters of proportional representation in this country. The arithmetical calculations that it requires can appear quite complicated but a simple example (see 2.10) can illustrate how it operates. It is more important to remember what the system achieves rather than the detailed workings of the mathematics.

ACTIVITY 9

A The STV system would mean that large multi-member constituencies would be created. Oxfordshire, for example, which currently elects five MPs from separate constituencies, would probably be a single constituency with the same number of MPs. What do you think might be the advantages and disadvantages of such an arrangement?

B The system allows voters to choose not only between parties but also between candidates of the same party. What might be the implications for the parties and for the electorate?

C How might this system favour some of the existing parties?

D The STV system can be seen to allow a more sophisticated choice for the voters but is also more complicated than our current system because the voting and counting is more complex. How important is this as an issue when deciding on the best voting system?

E What other advantages or problems might the introduction of STV bring?

Single Transferable Vote

2.10

In this system each constituency has a number of seats in the legislature. Like the Alternative Vote system, voters list candidates in order of preference. In the Killaloe constituency, there are five candidates competing for three seats.

Four candidates could get 150 votes but only three could get 151 or more. So you divide the votes cast by the seats available plus one (3 + 1) and add one to the answer.

600 Votes cast
÷ 4 Seats + 1
150

There are 600 voters and three seats, so a candidate needs at least 151 votes to win a seat. This number is worked out as shown above. The chart below shows how votes are allocated and who wins the seats.

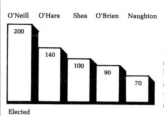

1. Voters list the candidates in order of preference on their ballot papers. The first choices only are then counted up. The totals of all the first choices are shown on the left.

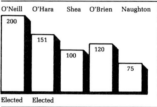

2. O'Neill has 49 more votes than her necessary minimum of 151. These are shared out in proportion to the second preferences on her ballot papers. These are as follows: O'Brien – 30, O'Hara – 11, Naughton – 8. The new totals are shown on the left.

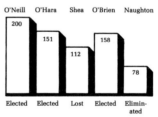

3. O'Hara has no surplus votes and the third representative has not yet been elected. So the losing candidate, Naughton, is eliminated and the second choices on his ballot papers are added up. Of these, O'Neill gets 20, O'Hara 8, Shea 12 and O'Brien 38. The final result of the election is shown on the left.

Source: J. Cooke and S. Kirby, adapted from *Introduction to politics and government*, Usborne, 1986

Elections in **Northern Ireland** to the Stormont Parliament between 1922 and 1928, the Assembly in 1973 and 1982, the Convention in 1975 and the European Parliament in 1984 have all used the **single transferable vote**. This system has been used because of the important division between Catholic and Protestant voters and the effect that has on voting behaviour.

ACTIVITY 10

A From what you already know of STV explain why successive governments have run some elections in Northern Ireland using this system.

B From 2.12 identify the Catholic/Nationalist and Protestant/Unionist parties.

C Did the 1982 election produce a proportionately elected Assembly?

D What is meant (2.12) by the phrase 'the party (SDLP) had lost its exclusive right to speak for the minority'?

E Why did the Official Unionists and the Democratic Unionists transfer their voting preferences between themselves, and with what consequences?

F Compare the results of the Assembly elections (2.12) with those for the 1987 General Election (2.11). What would you say is the major difference between them?

2.11
1987 General Election results in Northern Ireland

	VOTES	% SHARE	CANDIDATES	MPs ELECTED
Ulster Unionist	276,230	37.8	12	9
Democratic Unionist	85,642	11.7	4	3
Popular Unionist	18,420	2.5	1	1
SDLP	154,087	21.1	13	3
Sinn Fein	83,389	11.4	14	1
Alliance	72,671	10.0	16	—
Workers Party	19,294	2.6	14	—
Others	20,419	2.8	3	—

Source: *Fact sheet 47*, Public Information Office, House of Commons.

Results of the Northern Ireland Assembly elections, 1982   2.12

PARTY	NO. OF FIRST PREFERENCE VOTES	PERCENTAGE OF FIRST PREFERENCE VOTES	NO. OF CANDIDATES ELECTED
Official Ulster Unionists	188,277	29.7	26
Democratic Unionists	145,528	23.0	21
Social Democratic and Labour Party	118,891	18.8	14
Alliance Party	58,851	9.3	10
Sinn Fein	64,191	10.1	5
Other Unionists	24,418	3.9	2
Workers Party	17,216	2.7	0
United Ulster Unionists	11,550	1.8	0
Total	633,120	100	78

Source: F. Magee, *Northern Ireland since 1979*, Longman, 1984

Sinn Fein gained 10.1% of the vote and 5 seats thus breaking the SDLP's monopoly as representatives of the minority.

The SDLP share of the vote (18.8%) held up well. It was higher than its share in the 1981 local government elections when it had gained 17.6% of the vote. However, with 14 seats this was three fewer than in 1975 (Convention elections) and 5 fewer than in 1973 (Assembly and power-sharing executive). Its total vote was also down from 160,000 in 1973 to 118.891 in 1982. Most importantly, the party had lost its exclusive right to speak for the minority.

Unionist rivalry, especially between the two main Unionist parties, the Official Unionists and the Democratic Unionists, was strong. The Official Unionists share of the vote at 29.7% was up from 26.5% at the 1981 local elections whereas the DUP share at 23% had fallen from 26.6% in 1981. However, both parties transferred later preferences between them thereby gaining about 3 seats more than their proportionate share.

The Alliance Party share of the vote at 9.3% was up on the 8.8% they gained in the 1981 local elections, but their total vote has been declining from 66,541 in 1973 to 58,851 in 1982.

ACTIVITY 11

A It is argued that the list system (see data 2.13) strengthens the control of political parties. In what ways?

B Why is it usually necessary for parties to win a minimum percentage of the popular vote before winning seats?

C Look back to the votes that the parties won in the General Election of 1987 (data 2.3). Assuming a list system of voting and that the number of seats would have been exactly proportionate to the percentage of the votes cast for each party, what would the UK election result have been in numbers of seats for each party?

2.13

The List System

The most basic form of PR is the national list system. Each party, group or individual that wishes to stand for election presents a list of candidates. A list can, in certain variations of the system, consist of only one name, thus enabling individuals to stand.

Voters throughout the whole country vote for one or other of these lists. Seats in the legislature are shared out according to the votes obtained by each party list. If, for example, there are 100 seats in the legislature, and party A gets 40 per cent of the vote, party B 25 per cent, party C 20 per cent and party D 15 per cent, then they will get 40, 25, 20 and 15 seats respectively. The top 40 candidates on the list of party A will be declared elected, as will the top 25 on the list of party B, the top 20 on party C's list and the top 15 on party D's list.

This system normally produces coalition governments, and often unstable governments, as it is rare for one party to get more than 50 per cent of the vote, and small or minute parties may make the government fall by changing their allegiance from the governing coalition to the opposition. It encourages new and small parties by giving them parliamentary representation if they can muster enough votes in the whole country to justify a seat; their elected members can 'sell' their support to one of the bigger parties or to the governing coalition in exchange for policy compromises.

The system is useful when parties are based not only on political opinions but on religious or tribal differences. It enables voters to express their political preference *and* to vote for a tribal or religious party. In Belgium, for example, there are Flemish and Walloon Christian Democrat, Socialist and Liberal parties, as well as Flemish Nationalist Communist and Francophone or French-speakers' parties. After the election, the different parties of similar viewpoint tend to band together and co-operate in parliament.

This is, however, the least democratic of so-called democratic electoral systems. It is normally a small group at the top of the party hierarchy that decides who gets on the list of candidates and where on the list they should be. Candidates put at or near the top of major parties' lists are certain of election, while those at the bottom are equally certain of not being elected. The elector has only a very marginal influence in deciding the exact proportions between parties.

Source: A. Maude and J. Szemerey, *Why electoral change? The case for P.R. examined, Conservative Central Office*

In **Israel** the **list system** is used with each party having to gain only 1% of the popular vote to win seats. The Israeli General Election of 1988 produced the results shown in 2.15 which reflect the popular vote translated into seats. The two main parties in Israel are the Labour Party and the Likud.

ACTIVITY 12

A   To what extent do the figures in 2.15 justify the conclusions reached in the Guardian editorial (2.14)?

B   What does the editorial mean when it claims the Israeli election system allows 'the dogmatic tail to wag the secular dog'?

C   What solution does The Guardian propose to the problem of fragmentation and stalemate in Israeli politics?

2.14

Overdoing equality

IT WAS Abba Eban who observed that elections in Israel were about deciding who was to be allowed to share power with the religious minority parties. It is no joke now that four such groupings have won a total of 18 seats (and other fringe-groups eight) in a Knesset of 120 members, thus holding the balance of power. The price of the religious fringe for joining a coalition with the Likud or Labour includes the education, religious and interior ministries as well as more orthodox-Jewish regulation of daily life. Such impositions affect all citizens, regardless of religious commitment, of a state which is ethnically Jewish but constitutionally secular . . .

The nub (of the problem) is the low threshold, one per cent of the total vote, for entry into the Knesset.

The Swedes set the hurdle at three per cent, freshly surmounted by their Green Party at this year's election. This would be a happy medium to imitate from a country with unimpeachable credentials. The trick is to steer a fair course between giving all possible minorities in a fissiparous country a voice and respecting the right of the vast majority, regardless of party, to stable government . . .

Unrefined, the Israeli electoral system allows the dogmatic tail to wag the secular dog, a highly dangerous distortion in the democracy at the epicentre of the world's most politically sensitive and potentially explosive region.

Source: *The Guardian*, 8.11.88

2.15

THE SHAPE OF THE NEW KNESSET

BLOCKS AND PARTIES		1988	1984	1981
JEWISH SECULAR RIGHT				
KACH (extreme, racialist)		—	1	—
MOLEDET (favours "transfer" of Palestinians to Arab countries)		2	—	—
TSOMET (headed by ex-Chief of Staff; pro Ariel Sharon)		2	—	—
TEHIYA (opposed Camp David; hardline for "Greater Israel")		4	5	3
OTHERS		—	—	2
LIKUD		39	41	48
	TOTAL	47	47	53
RELIGIOUS				
MAFCAL NATIONAL RELIGIOUS PARTY (orthodox, pragmatic)		5	4	6
SHAS (ultra-orthodox, Sephardi, non-Zionist)		6	4	—
AGUDA (ultra-orthodox, Ashkenazi, non-Zionist)		5	2	4
SPLINTER PARTIES		2	2	—
	TOTAL	18	12	10
CENTRE				
SHINUI MERKAZ (non-socialist, pro civil liberties)		2	3	2
OTHERS (YAHAD, TAMI, OMETZ)		—	5	3
	TOTAL	2	8	5
JEWISH LEFT				
LABOUR		38	44	47
MAPAM (kibbutz-based socialist)		3	—	—
CITIZEN RIGHTS (anti-rabbinical; pro women's and Arab rights)		5	3	1
	TOTAL	46	47	48
ARAB				
DEMOCRATIC ARAB (pro two-state solution)		1	—	—
PROGRESSIVE LIST FOR PEACE (mixed list, but Arab led)		1	2	—
CHADASH – DEMOCRATIC FRONT (Palestinian, pro-Soviet)		5	4	4
	TOTAL	7	6	4

Source: *The Guardian*, 3.11.88

C. Reform of the British electoral system?

The strength of Conservative parliamentary majorities in elections since 1979 has led some commentators (2.17) to suggest Britain now has a 'dominant party system'. Those who favour electoral reform argue that the only way to break what they see as monopoly control of state power is by introducing a more representative form of voting. They point to models from other countries as the basis for their proposals.

In reality, whether or not electoral reform is introduced will depend not so much on the strength of the arguments but on political power. Under the present system the dominant party is likely to win the next election. Whilst they retain control of state power electoral reform is unlikely to happen. In other words, it is more a matter of political expediency than the debate of principle.

ACTIVITY 14

A What is the cartoonist suggesting in data 2.16?

B What do you think Patrick Dunleavy means when he says that 'Mrs Thatcher is poised to take control of state power and spread her ideas throughout the political system' (2.17)?

C According to Patrick Dunleavy a 'dominant party system' exists when 'a single party commands so large and so assured a share of the vote that it is permanently in government and can realistically never be beaten. The dominant party monopolises control over state power, and its influence progressively extends throughout virtually all other organs of the state (such as local government or supposedly independent institutions). Its ideology suffuses the political system and sets the terms of the debate.'

D Give two examples of how the Conservative Governments since 1979 have acted in ways that Dunleavy describes.

E What are the consequences for electoral reform of a 'dominant party system'?

Send her victorious 2.16

Source: *New Statesman and Society,* 16.9.88

ACTIVITY 15

Electoral reform is likely to remain an issue but whether or not it is ever achieved will probably depend on the balance of political power rather than the intellectual arguments.

Imagine the following political scenarios after the next general election:

1 another large Conservative majority,
2 a very small Conservative majority,
3 a 'hung' parliament,
4 a minority Labour Government,
5 a majority Labour Government,
6 A Democrat/SDP/Labour coalition.

What would be the likely consequences for electoral reform in each of these scenarios?

2.17

The argument for Britain's unfair voting system is that it delivers strong and stable government. So it does: overwhelmingly strong and stable Tory government. Historically, it's provided secure Tory majorities four times more often than Labour and made the Conservatives one of the most successful right-wing parties in the west. Now, argues Patrick Dunleavy, Mrs Thatcher is poised to take monopoly control of state power and spread her ideas throughout the political system. The SDP and SLD see the need for electoral reform. It's high time Labour did too.

Source: *New Statesman and Society,* 16.9.88

D. Conclusion

In this unit, you will have explored the way our present electoral system operates, considered alternatives and asked questions about the purpose of elections. You will have also thought about the consequences of maintaining the present system as well as the consequences of reform. The unit should have demonstrated that the issue of electoral reform is more complicated than it might at first appear and that there are vested interests in both arguments for change and arguments for retention of the present system. It should also be clear that whether change occurs will be more to do with the realities of political power and interests than with abstract notions of democracy or fairness.

Further reading

Vernon Bogdanor, *What is Proportional Representation,* Martin Robertson, 1984

Peter Hain, *Proportional Misrepresentation,* Wildwood House, 1986

Iain McLean, *Elections,* Longman, 2nd edition, 1980

Social Studies Review, *Choosing Representatives: Majority Electoral Systems,* Derek Urwin, March 1987

Social Studies Review, *Electing Representatives: Proportional Systems,* Derek Urwin, May 1987

Martin Harrop and William Miller, *Elections and Voters,* Macmillan, 1987

UNIT 3 Voting Behaviour

The 1987 General Election produced a third term for Margaret Thatcher's Conservative Government. Is this part of an irreversible trend in voting behaviour? Regional, gender, ethnic and social class differences may all contribute to understanding the way people vote. This unit explores these factors.

Introduction

Psephology, the study of voting behaviour, is not an exact science. Initially, at least, it is based on common sense observations. This unit concentrates on an analysis of voting statistics relating to recent British general elections. Trends in the number and percentage of votes cast can be identified from an examination of relevant voting statistics. The success with which parties can turn votes into seats in Parliament is, however, another matter.

ACTIVITY 1

Examine the data in 3.1.

A Describe what happened to the Conservative vote, and its representation in Parliament, between 1974 and 1987.
B Do the same for
   (i) the Labour Party
   (ii) the Liberal Party (for 1983 and 1987, use the 'Alliance' figures).
C Do these figures amount to a trend? Explain your answer.
D Disregarding the 'Others', say which party is
   (i) the most successful
   (ii) the least successful
   in turning votes into seats.

3.1

General Elections 1974–1987

Date	Party	Number of votes (millions)	Number of seats won	Percentage of votes	Percentage seats won
Feb 1974	Conservative	11.9	297	37.9	46.8
	Labour	11.6	301	37.1	47.4
	Liberal	6.1	14	19.3	2.2
	Others	1.8	23	5.6	3.6
Oct 1974	Conservative	10.5	277	35.8	43.6
	Labour	11.5	319	39.2	50.2
	Liberal	5.3	13	18.3	2.1
	Others	1.9	26	6.6	4.2
1979	Conservative	15.7	339	43.9	53.4
	Labour	11.5	268	36.9	42.2
	Liberal	4.3	11	13.8	1.7
	Others	1.7	17	5.5	2.7
1983	Conservative	13.0	397	42.4	61.1
	Labour	8.5	209	27.6	32.2
	Alliance	7.8	23	25.4	3.5
	Others	1.4	21	4.6	3.2
1987	Conservative	13.7	375	42.3	57.6
	Labour	10.0	228	30.8	35.2
	Alliance	7.3	22	22.6	3.5
	Others	1.3	23	4.3	3.5

A. Regional differences

This section examines the view that voting behaviour is influenced by where the voter lives. Commentators have recently stressed the importance of a divide between North and South. The possibility of a link between affluence and regionalism is examined by comparing the distribution of wealth (3.3–3.5) with the share of the vote in the 1987 election (3.2).

ACTIVITY 2

Data 3.2 shows the respresentation of the parties in Parliament, by region, following the 1987 General Election.

A Which party did well in the North and Scotland?
B In which regions did the Liberal-SDP Alliance do well?
C Is there sufficient evidence to confirm the view that there is a divide between North and South in terms of party support?

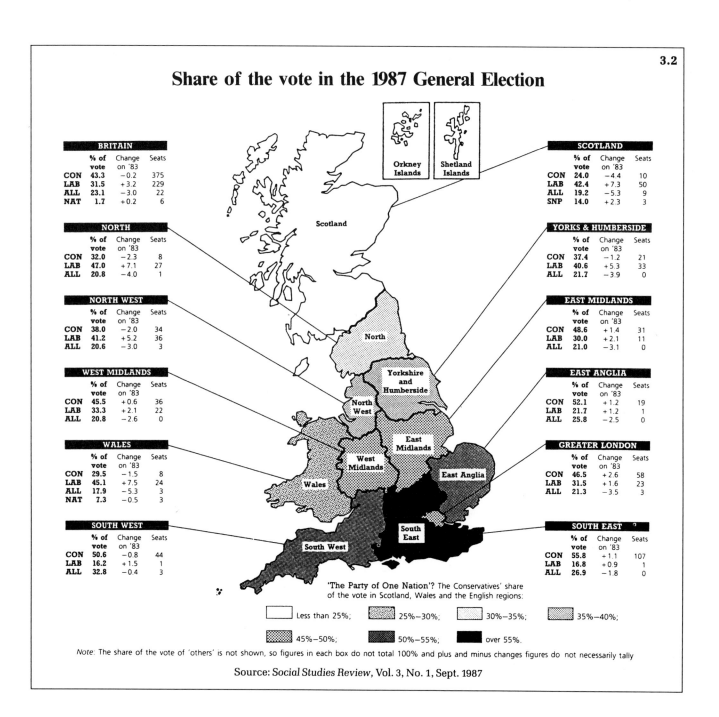

Share of the vote in the 1987 General Election

3.2

BRITAIN

	% of vote	Change on '83	Seats
CON	43.3	−0.2	375
LAB	31.5	+3.2	229
ALL	23.1	−3.0	22
NAT	1.7	+0.2	6

NORTH

	% of vote	Change on '83	Seats
CON	32.0	−2.3	8
LAB	47.0	+7.1	27
ALL	20.8	−4.0	1

NORTH WEST

	% of vote	Change on '83	Seats
CON	38.0	−2.0	34
LAB	41.2	+5.2	36
ALL	20.6	−3.0	3

WEST MIDLANDS

	% of vote	Change on '83	Seats
CON	45.5	+0.6	36
LAB	33.3	+2.1	22
ALL	20.8	−2.6	0

WALES

	% of vote	Change on '83	Seats
CON	29.5	−1.5	8
LAB	45.1	+7.5	24
ALL	17.9	−5.3	3
NAT	7.3	−0.5	3

SOUTH WEST

	% of vote	Change on '83	Seats
CON	50.6	−0.8	44
LAB	16.2	+1.5	1
ALL	32.8	−0.4	3

SCOTLAND

	% of vote	Change on '83	Seats
CON	24.0	−4.4	10
LAB	42.4	+7.3	50
ALL	19.2	−5.3	9
SNP	14.0	+2.3	3

YORKS & HUMBERSIDE

	% of vote	Change on '83	Seats
CON	37.4	−1.2	21
LAB	40.6	+5.3	33
ALL	21.7	−3.9	0

EAST MIDLANDS

	% of vote	Change on '83	Seats
CON	48.6	+1.4	31
LAB	30.0	+2.1	11
ALL	21.0	−3.1	0

EAST ANGLIA

	% of vote	Change on '83	Seats
CON	52.1	+1.2	19
LAB	21.7	+1.2	1
ALL	25.8	−2.5	0

GREATER LONDON

	% of vote	Change on '83	Seats
CON	46.5	+2.6	58
LAB	31.5	+1.6	23
ALL	21.3	−3.5	3

SOUTH EAST

	% of vote	Change on '83	Seats
CON	55.8	+1.1	107
LAB	16.8	+0.9	1
ALL	26.9	−1.8	0

'The Party of One Nation'? The Conservatives' share of the vote in Scotland, Wales and the English regions:

Less than 25%;   25%–30%;   30%–35%;   35%–40%;
45%–50%;   50%–55%;   over 55%.

Note: The share of the vote of 'others' is not shown, so figures in each box do not total 100% and plus and minus changes figures do not necessarily tally

Source: *Social Studies Review*, Vol. 3, No. 1, Sept. 1987

ACTIVITY 3
Compare the data in 3.2 with those in 3.3–3.5.
Is there a relationship between 'regional affluence' and voting? If so, which parties benefit from the more affluent regions? How might such a link be explained?

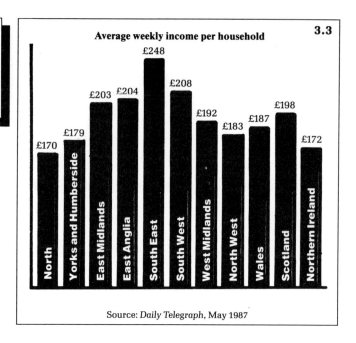

3.3

Average weekly income per household

North	£170
Yorks and Humberside	£179
East Midlands	£203
East Anglia	£204
South East	£248
South West	£208
West Midlands	£192
North West	£183
Wales	£187
Scotland	£198
Northern Ireland	£172

Source: *Daily Telegraph*, May 1987

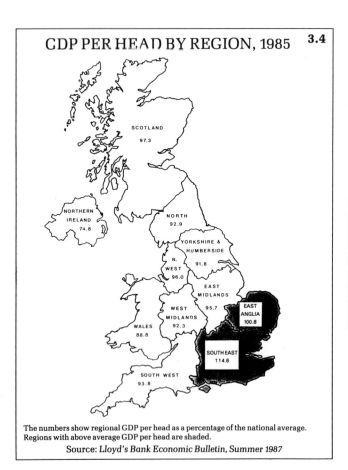

GDP PER HEAD BY REGION, 1985   **3.4**

SCOTLAND 97.3

NORTHERN IRELAND 74.8

NORTH 92.9

YORKSHIRE & HUMBERSIDE 91.8

N. WEST 96.0

EAST MIDLANDS 95.7

WEST MIDLANDS 92.3

EAST ANGLIA 100.8

WALES 88.8

SOUTH EAST 114.6

SOUTH WEST 93.8

The numbers show regional GDP per head as a percentage of the national average.
Regions with above average GDP per head are shaded.
Source: *Lloyd's Bank Economic Bulletin*, Summer 1987

3.5

Regional performance. Ranked by gdp per head.

	Gdp per head 1985	Personal disposable Income per head, 1985	Real personal disposable Income growth per head, 1975–85	Unemployment % of working population Jan 1987	Long term unemployed % of unemployed Jan 1987
South East	5831	4725	19.92	8.5	36.2
East Anglia	5118	4244	26.21	9.3	33.5
Scotland	4942	4181	20.86	15.1	39.2
North West	4877	4074	16.95	14.3	44.3
E. Midlands	4861	4066	18.46	11.4	39.2
South West	4763	4152	21.34	10.4	32.7
North	4717	3919	18.24	16.9	44.3
W. Midlands	4690	3997	10.24	13.8	46.3
Yorks & Humb	4662	3923	17.70	13.8	42.0
Wales	4509	3778	14.27	14.3	40.6
N. Ireland	3799	3538	18.67	19.3	50.0

Source: *Economic Trends, Employment Gazette, Lloyds Bank Economic Bulletin*, May 1987

The Labour Party has generally done well in the North, the Conservatives in the South, and the parties of the centre have been quite good at coming second in many regions. In order to gain more seats, the former Alliance parties needed to convince Conservative voters in the North and Labour voters in the South to vote for them as the next best choice. This is known as 'tactical voting'.

ACTIVITY 4

Consider the evidence from the 1987 General Election in data 3.6.

A Did significant numbers of people vote tactically in 1987?

B Which parties 'lost' votes, and to whom, in the tactical competition for votes?

C In what way may this accentuate the apparent divide between North and South, as reflected in voting behaviour?

3.6

Q: Did you vote for your first-choice party; or did you vote tactically, to defeat another party?

	All	Con	Lab	Lib/SDP
· Voted for party/ candidate of first choice	81	88	81	77
· Voted tactically	17	11	17	28

Source: ITN/Harris Exit Poll

B. Gender differences

It has traditionally been thought that a higher proportion of women than men vote Conservative. Recent psephological evidence, however, now challenges this view.

ACTIVITY 5

Using data 3.7–3.8, list the arguments and evidence which suggest that women are no longer more likely to support the Conservative Party.

3.7

Party support by gender

	Con	Lab	Lib/SDP	Others
ALL	43.3{ – 0.2}	31.6{ + 3.3}	23.1{ – 2.9}	2.0{ – 0.2}
Sex:				
MEN	41{0}	33{ + 3}	23{ – 3}	3{ – 1}
WOMEN	43{ – 1}	31{ + 3}	23{ – 3}	3{ + 1}

Changes since 1983 in brackets
Source: ITN/Harris Exit Poll, *op. cit.*

3.8

Why do women vote Tory?

Psephologists and political scientists have tended to assume that women vote Conservative because they are naturally conservative. But if we rely on 'natural causes' as the explanation, how are we to explain, for example, that in the United States the gender gap is working the other way, in favour of the Democrats? In any case, it doesn't explain the tendency for a higher proportion of women voters in Britain to support the Tories, nor the variations among women of different ages, classes (their own rather than husbands') and domestic circumstances. We shall see that until recently these questions have not been addressed by straight psephologists (students of voting) who have tended to see women's sex as sufficient explanation. But complex and apparently contradictory features appear when we look at women's *political* as well as their *party* orientations. We will see that something seems to be afoot among women – they may not be the conservative sex in the future and already on any social-political issues women tend to be the more radical sex.

Men and women on the move

We now know that, despite the conventional wisdom, in no simple sense was it women who elected Margaret Thatcher's governments in 1979 and 1983. Despite some divergences in the statistics produced by different polling organisations, they showed that the most dramatic swing towards the Conservatives was among men.

MORI swing to the Conservatives:	men 7 per cent, women 5.5 per cent
BBC/Gallup	men 9.5 per cent, women 3 per cent

1985 (July–September)	men	women	gender gap
Con	31	32	+ 1
Lab	37	34	– 3
Alliance	30	32	+ 2

Shortly before Cruise missiles arrived in the winter of 1983, there was, according to the political columnist, Peter Kellner, a 34-point gender gap. That gender gap was 'the largest, as far as I am aware that any poll has ever found on any major political issue'. By 1986 the nuclear agenda had broadened, and still there was a significant gender gap:

Gallup August 1986	Men	Women
UK should get rid of nuclear arms, whatever anyone else does	39	49
should not	54	39
nuclear arms do not keep you safe	53	47
for phasing out nuclear power	48	56
against phase-out	45	24

Source: Beatrix Campbell, *The Iron Ladies: Why do Women Vote Tory?*, Virago, 1987

C. Ethnic differences

Ethnic communities have in the past allied themselves with the Labour Party. There is some evidence though that this support may be fragmenting. Opinion polls allow us to analyse this trend by ethnic group (3.10, 3.11). Data 3.12 and 3.13 look at possible reasons for any changes, and 3.14 presents a somewhat different interpretation of past and possible future trends.

ACTIVITY 6

Study data 3.9–3.14 which attempt to show and explain possible changes in the voting patterns of ethnic minorities.

A   Which parties are supported by which ethnic groups?

B   What changes in the voting patterns of ethnic minorities appear to have taken place since the 1979 General Election?

C   What possible explanations are provided for such changes?

D   Read data 3.14.

   (i)   In what ways does Zig Layton-Henry's analysis differ from the other data in this section?

   (ii) What expectations does the author have about the future voting behaviour of the black electorate? How far do you agree with the reasons he gives to support these views?

3.9

Young, affluent and Asian. How long can Labour hold this vote?

Source: Lynton Robins, *Talking Politics*, Vol. 1, no. 1

3.10

Black support for Labour slipping, poll indicates

BLACK SUPPORT for the Labour Party appears to be slipping, according to the latest poll of ethnic minority voters.

A poll carried out for the Hansib group of newspapers – *Asian Times, Caribbean Times*, and *African Times* – by the Harris Research Centre gives Labour 72 per cent, Conservatives 18 per cent and the Alliance 10 per cent.

But surveys for the Commission for Racial Equality gave Labour stronger black support in the 1979 and 1983 general elections.

The latest poll shows strongest support for Labour in the West Indian community, with Labour on 86 per cent, Conservatives, 6 per cent and the Alliance 7 per cent. The CRE figures suggest that Labour had 90 per cent of the Afro-Caribbean vote in 1979, but 86 per cent in the last election.

The fall would appear to have been in the Asian vote. The CRE surveys gave Labour 86 per cent of the Asian vote in 1979, 80 per cent in 1983 but the latest poll of Asian voters gives Labour 67 per cent, Conservatives, 23 per cent and Alliance 10.

Source: *The Independent*, May 1987

3.11

Labour share of two-party support, by class and age within ethnic groups, February 1978

	WHITE %	AFRO-CARIBBEAN %	ASIAN %
SOCIAL CLASS			
AB, C1	24	90	86
C2	49	94	93
D, E	63	99	97
AGE			
16–34	48	96	90
35–54	43	92	93
55+	40	100*	100*
ALL	44	95	92
sample	(1,416)	(233)	(256)

*No. too small for statistical significance

Source: Ivor Crewe, *New Society*

3.12

The affluent Asian voter

BRITAIN'S immigrant community is much too young for it to have achieved representation on every rung of the meritocratic ladder. But several sections of the black community have discovered the joys of upward mobility. There are those who make it through money. The Asians can count a few hundred millionaires and a few thousand more who've moved commercially from pocket calculator to computer. They vote Tory or SDP and will do in increasing numbers, bringing with them the 'cultural' and religious organisations which aren't antipathetic to the ethic of Victorian family values and business.

Source: Farrukh Dhondy, *New Statesman*

3.13

A move away from Labour?

WHAT ABOUT the black voters themselves? They have, so far, been remarkably loyal to the Labour Party. At the last election, about two-thirds of them voted Labour, compared to only 28 per cent of the whole electorate. With such a high proportion of the black vote already, Labour is unlikely to get more. So even if Black Sections were now to be introduced, Labour might not win more black votes – just lose fewer of them.

For Labour cannot afford to take the black vote for granted. Immigrants, when they first come to Britain, tend to vote Labour, mainly because they are economically and socially disadvantaged. As they become more integrated into society, their voting patterns become more like the rest of the population. That is what happened with Jewish immigrants earlier this century; and what is just starting to happen with Asians now. A GLC survey in 1984 found that Asians in the top socio-economic group were twice as likely as whites to have changed the party they voted for between 1979 and 1983. Afro-Caribbeans may take rather longer to switch allegiance, but the danger is still there.

Source: Mary Ann Sieghart, *New Statesman*

3.14

Black support for the Labour Party

The General Election of 1987 shows a consolidation of black support for the Labour Party which has no doubt been reinforced by the election of four black Labour MPs.

The much-heralded shift among black voters, especially Asians, towards the Conservatives, is as yet unproven. In the future, one would expect that class voting will increase among members of the black electorate but there are many reasons why this is likely to be very slow. These include the continued determination of Mrs Thatcher's government to tighten immigration controls, the lack of sympathy for anti-discrimination measures, the attacks on inner-city authorities, the disproportionately adverse effect of the poll tax on black families, especially in inner-city areas, and the willingness of the government to allow the Labour party to be identified with what the Conservatives regard as unpopular minorities.

Source: Zig Layton-Henry, 'Black participation in the general election of 1987', *Talking Politics*, Vol 1, No 1, Autumn, 1988, pp. 20–24

D. Social class differences

Social class has been seen as a very significant factor in determining how people vote. Although at least one third of the working class has traditionally voted Conservative, Labour has been viewed as the party of the working class and the Conservatives as the party of the middle class. More recently, the centre parties such as Democrats and SDP have been seen as drawing support from across all classes.

These commonly held views are examined here. There are contradictory interpretations of the relationship between social class and voting behaviour and different methods of classification are used.

Data 3.15 shows a conventional method of defining social class according to occupational categories. The boundary between the middle class and the working class is traditionally drawn between C1 and C2. 3.16 shows an alternative method of classifying the working class.

ACTIVITY 7

A What conclusions can be drawn from 3.15 about class support for the different parties at the 1987 election?

B Using data 3.16:
  (i) How does Ivor Crewe distinguish between the 'traditional working class' and the 'new working class'?
  (ii) What conclusions might be drawn about working class support for the Labour Party?

C If the trends outlined in 3.17 continue, which party or parties seem likely to benefit in future elections? Explain your answer by referring also to 3.16.

3.15

1987 General Election (%)

CLASS GROUP		CONS	LAB	ALLIANCE
AB	(professional/managerial)	57	14	26
C1	(white collar)	51	21	26
C2	(skilled workers)	40	36	22
DE	(semi-skilled/unskilled)	30	48	20

Source: Mori

3.16

The divided working class: the parties' shares of the vote among different groups of manual workers (%)

Party	THE NEW WORKING CLASS				THE TRADITIONAL WORKING CLASS			
	Lives in South	Home-Owner	Non-Union Member	Private Sector Worker	Lives in Scotland or North	Council Tenant	Union Member	Public Sector Worker
CONS.	46	44	40	38	29	25	30	32
LAB.	28	32	38	39	57	57	48	49
LIB/SDP Alliance	26	24	22	23	15	18	22	19

Source: 'Why Mrs. Thatcher was returned with a landslide', Ivor Crewe, *Social Studies Review*, Vol. 3, No. 1, September, 1987

3.17

Government policies are producing a steady expansion of the new working class, and a diminution of the old. Council house sales, privatisation, the decline of manufacturing industry (on which the old unions are based) and the steady population drift to the South are continuing to restructure the working class.

Source: Crewe, *op. cit.*

After the 1983 election, Ivor Crewe had claimed: 'The Labour vote remains largely working class; but the working class ceased to be largely Labour.' Other writers, too, have argued that the link between social class and voting behaviour has been breaking down. This process has been called **class dealignment**. Not all political scientists accept this argument, saying that it depends partly on how social class is defined and how the electorate is classified.

In 3.18 Heath, Jowell and Curtice provide a further way of categorizing the electorate on class lines. The percentage vote for the main parties at the 1983 election, from each of the different classes, is also shown. These authors accept that the working class has declined as a proportion of the total electorate. But they argue that the proportion of working class people voting Labour has not declined: class dealignment has not taken place. The percentage of the working class voting Labour was as high in 1987 (when Labour lost) as it was in 1966 (when Labour won).

ACTIVITY 8

A   What conclusions can be drawn from 3.18 about class support for the different parties at the 1983 election?

B   Show how Heath, Jowell and Curtice's account of the working class differs from Crewe's in terms of:
   (i)   their method of classification
   (ii) their conclusions about class dealignment.

3.18

Heath, Jowell and Curtice: five classes

1. **The salariat** – managers and administrators, supervisors of nonmanual workers, professionals and semi-professionals.
2. **Routine nonmanual** – e.g. clerks, salesworkers and secretaries.
3. **The petty bourgeoisie** – farmers, small proprietors and self-employed manual workers.
4. **Foremen and technicians**.
5. **The working class** – rank and file manual employees: no distinction between skilled and semi-skilled

Class and party support, 1983 General Election

	CON	LAB	LIB/SDP
Salariat	54	14	31
Routine nonmanual	46	25	27
Petty bourgeoisie	71	12	17
Foremen/technicians	48	26	25
Working class	30	49	20

Source: *How Britain Votes*, A. Heath, R. Jowell, J. Curtice, Pergamon, Oxford, 1983

After Labour had lost its third successive election in 1959, a commonly expressed explanation was that the working class had become too small for Labour, as the 'working class party', to win elections. Partly because of higher wages, improved living standards and the services provided by the Welfare State, more and more people were becoming 'middle class', it was claimed. Consequently they were switching their support to the 'middle class party': the Conservatives. This explanation was referred to as the **embourgeoisement thesis**. A similar argument – that increased 'affluence' leads to increased support for the Tory Party – has accompanied some of the theories about class dealignment.

ACTIVITY 9

How do the comments of Doreen Massey in 3.19 differ from:

A   the conclusions of Heath, Jowell and Curtice?
B   the embourgeoisement thesis?

ACTIVITY 10

Taking in turn the positions adopted by

A Crewe
B Heath, Jowell and Curtice
C Massey

suggest, in each case, what the Labour Party should do to capture a larger slice of the vote at the next general election.

3.19

Self-interest

The divide in the 1987 election was not a class divide. More, it was about immediate self-interest. The evidence is that the best predictor of how individuals would vote was whether they thought the economy had got better or worse, and what they perceived as happening to their living-standards. In other words, people of all classes who are doing well out of Thatcherism, or even who think they may, voted Tory. This cuts across the deeper social divisions. The temptation to buy your council house is far greater in the South where prices are rocketing, than in the North. So, with over 3m unemployed and manufacturing output still lower than in 1979, the Conservatives won the economic argument. Enough people feel they are doing OK.

Source: 'Heartlands of defeat', Doreen Massey, *Marxism Today*, July, 1987

E. Conclusion

This unit has focussed on some of the possible longer-term trends and changes in the patterns of voting behaviour according to region, gender, ethnicity and class. At the outset, it was emphasised that psephology is not an exact science, and many other variables – including shorter-term factors – may combine in affecting the outcome of a general election. Specific events, issues and policies, the styles of the party leaders, the publication and use of opinion poll findings, and the role of the mass media may all be significant. Some of these factors are explored further in other units of this book.

ACTIVITY 11

What does the cartoon (3.20) suggest about the influence of some of the shorter-term factors referred to in the Conclusion?

3.20

Source: Private Eye, no 666, 26.6.87

Further Reading

Benyon, J. 'A prolonged Conservative ascendancy in a divided Britain?' *Social Studies Review* Vol. 3, No. 1, 1987
Crewe, I. 'Why Mrs Thatcher was returned with a landslide' *Social Studies Review*, Vol. 3, No. 1, 1987
Curtice, J. 'Must Labour Lose' *New Society* 19.6.87
Heath, A., Jowell, R., Curtice, J. *How Britain Votes* Pergamon, Oxford, 1983
Jowell, R., Witherspoon, S., Brook, L. *British Social Attitudes, 1987* Gower, Aldershot, 1987 (Chapters 3 and 8)

UNIT 4 Politics and the Mass Media

Through an examination of the debates about ownership and control, media bias, political satire, the use of stereotypes and the future of broadcasting, this unit encourages an exploration of some of the central questions about the relationships between the mass media and politics.

Introduction

In societies like Britain 'politics' is a very specialised activity. Most of us are not politicians. Indeed, apart perhaps from a brief handshake at election time, most of us have not even met a politician. Therefore, much of what we know of the world of politics – its customs, procedures and leading figures – we have learned secondhand from the *media*. Similarly most people lack either first hand experience or specialised knowledge of many of the matters with which politicians deal. By no means everyone, for instance, belongs to a trade union or an ethnic minority; or has lived in an inner city district, or been inside a prison, or engaged the Argentinian navy in the South Atlantic; or carries with him/her the latest trade figures, crime statistics or defence estimates. For our information about these things we rely, once again, almost solely upon the media. The citizens of this and other Western democracies may not actually be told *what* to think politically by the media, but they are told what to think politically *with*. This is why the media are important to study in relation to politics.

A. Coming together

At one time politicians strongly resisted any reporting of political affairs by the media. This section suggests that such resistance was to protect the monopoly over parliamentary business held by upper class males. Data 4.1–4.4 illustrate the struggle of the press to break down this monopoly.

ACTIVITY 1

A Using data 4.1 and 4.2, explain the reasons why Parliament opposed the reporting of parliamentary business by the newspapers in the eighteenth century.

B What methods were used to obstruct the press in reporting Parliament? (4.1)

C What do you think the 'pauper press' was (4.3) and why do you think it was especially resented by parliamentarians of the eighteenth and nineteenth centuries?

D Using data 4.1–4.4 construct an argument in favour of press freedom to report political affairs.

4.1

1649	Printing Act, regulated the press
1660–1	Parliament prohibited publication of its proceedings
1702	First daily newspaper, the *Daily Courant*, published
1712	'Taxes on knowledge' introduced (Advertisement Duty, Excise Duty on paper, and a tax on newspapers)
1725	Stamp Act: further regulation of newspapers
1738	Suppression of publication of parliamentary debates
1764	Prosecution of John Wilkes for seditious libel in the *North Briton*
1771	The House of Commons opened proceedings to the press
1775	The House of Lords did likewise
1802	Cobbett's *Weekly Political Register* founded
1817	*Black Dwarf* founded
1819	Six Acts, attacked the radical press
1830s	The so called 'War of the Unstamped'
1855	Stamp Duty abolished

Source: adapted from George Boyce, James Curran and Pauline Wingate (Editors), *Newspaper History: from the 17th century to the present day*, Constable, London, 1978, pp 407–8

4.2

Newspapers – a misfortune?

We have long considered the establishment of newspapers in this country as a misfortune to be regretted; but since their influence has become predominant by the universality of their circulation, we regard it as a calamity most deeply to be deplored.

Source: *Anti-Jacobin review*, 1801 (quoted in Raymond Williams, *The Long Revolution*, Pelican, p.208)

4.4

Freedom of the press?

The liberty of the press is the birthright of a Briton, and is justly esteemed the first bulwark of the liberties of this country.

Source: John Wilkes

4.3

THE
POOR MAN'S GUARDIAN,
A WEEKLY PAPER FOR THE PEOPLE.

This Paper (after sustaining a Government persecution of three years and a half duration, in which upwards of 500 persons were unjustly imprisoned, and cruelly treated for vending it) was, on the Trial of an Ex-Officio Information filed by

HIS MAJESTY'S ATTORNEY GENERAL against HENRY HETHERINGTON,

IN THE COURT OF ENCHEQUER,

Before LORD LYNDHURST *and a Special Jury,*

DECLARED TO BE

A STRICTLY LEGAL PUBLICATION.

Printed and Published by H. Hetherington, 126, Strand.

No. 161.]   *Saturday, July 5,* 1834.   [Price 1d.

PROGRESS OF DESPOTISM IN AMERICA.—THE MIDDLE CLASSES SHOWN TO BE THE REAL AUTHORS OF SLAVERY IN ALL NATIONS. READ AND LEARN, &c.

Friends, Brethren, and Fellow-Countrymen,

In these dreadful times when liberty is, as it were, hunted out of the world, when the best part of man-

In the Spring of 1989, MPs finally agreed to experiment with the televising of Common's proceedings, but only for a trial period and under strict conditions (see data 4.5). Opposition to the televising of Parliament has been less clearcut. For one thing, the existence of universal suffrage means that no one social class or gender group can exclude another from the mysteries of Parliament. This, however, does not stop those favourably inclined to the televising of Parliament using the argument that it extends democracy.

ACTIVITY 2

A   Extend data 4.6 and 4.7 by adding further arguments for **or** against the televising of Parliament.

B   Which, if any, of the arguments about TV coverage bear a resemblance to those in 4.1 to 4.3 about press reporting of Parliament?

C   Study 4.5. Propose a case for and one against these restrictions.

4.5

- MPs must be shown in head-and-shoulders shots only, not close-ups
- during questions, the camera must focus only on the questioner and on the Minister replying. Cut-away shots are only allowable if another MP is either being referred to or trying to intervene
- during any disorder, interruption or demonstration in the gallery the camera must focus on the Chair for the duration
- TV pictures of proceedings are not to be used in any light entertainment programmes, party political broadcasts, political satire shows, or any advertising/publicity material
- coverage 'should give an unvarnished account' of the work of the Commons, free of subjective commentary and editorialising. The television pictures, say MPs, should be left as far as possible to speak for themselves.

Source: First Report of the House of Commons Select Committee on *Televising of Proceedings of the House* Vol. 1 HMSO 1989

4.6

'The image of the individual woman standing at the dispatch box, with the men howling and shouting at her while she tries to give the impression that she is faced with enormous difficulties in running the country because of all the hooligans on the Opposition benches, will be worth half a million votes.'
Joe Ashton, Labour MP

'Ministers would make four statements a day and the front bench would monopolise debate. The back benches would end up something like Cecil B de Mille's chorus from Samson and Delilah.'
Joe Ashton, Labour MP

'The past generations of members who sit on these green benches are the holders of a trust ... which it is our duty to hand over as little as possible diminished to those who will sit here after us.'
Enoch Powell, Ulster Unionist, and former Conservative MP

Source: quoted by Bob Franklin, 'A Leap in the Dark: MPs' Objections to Televising Parliament', *Parliamentary Affairs*, July/September 1986

4.7

Advocates of broadcasting foresee ... substantial consequences flowing from a decision to televise the Commons. Television is considered a vital ingredient in a modern parliamentary democracy, capable of closing the communications gap between parliamentarians and citizens by educating and informing the latter. Television might also serve to halt the twentieth century decline of Parliament and save it from political obscurity by publicising its central role as a watchdog of government.

Source: Bob Franklin, TV Researcher, Leeds University

B. The media: ownership and control

This section hypothesises that the increasing concentration of ownership and control of the British media has meant a corresponding narrowing in the range of political ideas and viewpoints available to audiences.

With the one important exception of the BBC, established as a public corporation in 1926, the media in Britain are in private ownership and the pattern of this ownership is one of quite narrow concentration. Recent research shows that **multinational, multimedia conglomerates** – for example, the massive corporations controlled by Rupert Murdoch (News Corporation) and Robert Maxwell (Maxwell Communications Corporation) – have consolidated for themselves a huge share of each media market. For instance, three quarters of all daily, and four fifths of all Sunday, newspapers in Britain are owned by the top three ownership groups in each respective field. Such groups are likely to have similarly extensive holdings in other media: books, magazines, TV companies, radio stations, films, video, cable TV, satellite broadcasting and so on, across several countries.

ACTIVITY 3

A   Data 4.8 and 4.10 express very different viewpoints on where control of the media lies. What is the essential difference between them?

B   Identify these two views with those of each of the characters in the cartoon (4.9), explaining the connection in each case.

C   Explaining your answer, say which of the two views might be supported by the evidence in 4.11.

4.8

Their [the multimedia conglomerates] rise represents an unprecedented concentration of potential control over the production and flow of information and imagery. At the same time, the countervailing power of public intervention is being steadily weakened both institutionally, through the withdrawal of public ownership and subsidy, and philosophically, through the aggressive promotion of free market principles.

Source: Peter Golding and Graham Murdock, 'The new communications revolution', in James Curran et al (Editors), *Bending Reality*, Pluto Press, 1986

4.9

4.10

...the central truth about newspapers (is) that they are what they are because human nature is what it is. The speed at which most of their contents are written, and judged, means that they reflect certain human reactions with an undissembled [unconcealed] accuracy. Their content cannot exceed the capacity of their writers, clearly; but, even more limitingly, it cannot go beyond the range of their readers. It is therefore the readers, in the end, who are the figures of power.

Source: John Whale, *The Politics of the Media*, Fontana, 1977

4.11

Editorial recommendations for the outcome of the 1983 General Election

DAILIES		SUNDAYS	
Guardian	Small Conservative majority	Observer	Small Conservative majority
Times	Conservative	S.Telegraph	Conservative
D.Telegraph	Conservative	S.Times	Conservative
Daily Star	Conservative	Mail on Sunday	Conservative
Daily Express	Conservative	News of the World	Conservative
Daily Mirror	Labour	S.Express	Conservative
Sun	Conservative	S.Mirror	Labour
Financial Times	Conservative	S.People	Not Conservative

C. Bad news? Bias in television news coverage

ACTIVITY 4
What is the cartoonist in 4.12 trying to say about television news?

4.12

Are the media biased? If so, does this bias have political consequences? In both the media and academic worlds, the debate about media bias has been led since the mid-1970s by the Glasgow University Media Group which has produced five separate books on the subject. These publications concentrate on TV news which is bound by charter to be 'impartial'. They argue that we live in an unequal society divided by, among other things, class and gender and based upon a capitalist economic system. The ways of explaining day-to-day events in this society – be they in politics, industry or wherever, are numerous; but media explanations are invariably skewed toward certain assumptions. These assumptions are the basis of a consensus of opinion which prevails among the more powerful sections of society. The reasons for this skewing may be complex but the upshot is that explanations current among less powerful groups – trade unions, for example – will be treated with routine suspicion, or perhaps excluded altogether. Thus, in the now popular phrase, the media 'set the agenda'; determining to some extent what is discussed in the realm of politics and the terms of that discussion. Possibly the best way that the group found to illustrate their ideas succinctly was in 1977, when three of its members, Greg Philo, Peter Beharrel and John Hewitt, began a book about the depiction of trade unions in the media with a spoof of Independent Television News' *News At Ten*, substituting groups with high status and credibility for groups which, they argue, enjoy less of these commodities.

ACTIVITY 5
What point is being made by the *News at Ten spoof* (4.13)?

4.13

The alternative news?

The lamps in Parliament Square glisten across the Thames, the camera moves to Big Ben, a close-up, it's ten o'clock – Bong! – the familiar voice of Reginald Bosanquet – 'MP's pay rise endangers Social Contract (government agreement with trade unions on wages and prices)' – Bong! 'Royal Family squares up for massive wage claim' – Bong! – 'British Leyland's future threatened by huge dividend payouts' – Bong! – 'Traffic to be disrupted by Queen's Procession'....

Source: *Trade Unions and the Media*, P Beharrel and E Philo (ed), Macmillan, 1977

The publication of the *Bad News* books caused considerable anger in the television companies and a popular criticism of the Glasgow team was that, although they had made some valid points, they had failed to acknowledge their own biases and had dressed up left wing argument in scientific garb. A leading critic of the Glasgow work was Martin Harrison, Professor of Politics at Keele University. He analysed transcripts of news bulletins put out by ITN and studied by the Glasgow team. Harrison (see 4.14) took up one central point raised in the *Bad News* literature: the fact that industrial relations are usually reported in terms of strikes, and that strikes are invariably shown to have **effects** rather than **causes**.

ACTIVITY 6
Examine the arguments put forward in data 4.14

A   What point does Harrison seek to make about strikes?
B   How do the media use terms like 'hotheads' and 'mischief-makers' in their coverage of strikes?
C   Why do employers seem more skilful in avoiding the cameras than their union counterparts?
D   Harrison studied transcripts, but no film. In what ways may film coverage be 'biased'?
E   What implications does the debate over media bias have for party politics?

4.14

The reality of industrial life is that on any given day the vast majority of workplaces are operating normally, most workers rarely or never strike, and shop stewards' energies are directed more towards avoiding industrial action than to precipitating it. Yet strikes and the hotheads and mischief-makers that conflict tends to attract are also realities; the media did not invent... that ambulance drivers' spokesman who was prepared to let patients die if need be during the 1978–79 'winter of discontent'. Neither did they invent employers involved in confrontation with workers – though the more *neanderthal patrons de choc* [uncompromising members of management] seem more skilful at avoiding the cameras than their union counterparts.

Source: Martin Harrison, *TV News: Whose Bias?*, Policy Journals, 1985

ACTIVITY 7
Referring to data 4.15–4.16, argue a case for **or** against the view that there should be limits to impartiality of TV news.

4.15

'The BBC are taking it to the point of being impartial between the fire and the fire brigade.' Sir Winston Churchill

4.16

'Yes, we are biased – biased in favour of parliamentary democracy.' Sir Charles Curran, Director General, BBC, 1970s

D. Political satire

Popular contempt for politicians is centuries old, and we are all familiar with jokes made at their expense: 'You can always tell when a politician's lying. His lips move', 'Want to buy a politician's brain? Never been used', and so on. Starting around 1960, this kind of mockery of politicians began to influence popular comedy in Britain (see data 4.17–4.21).

ACTIVITY 8

A What is significant about the fact that the first TV satire programme (*That Was The Week That Was*) came from the BBC's current affairs section, rather than entertainment?

B What significance do you see in the fact that most of the early satirists were educated at Britain's two premier universities – Oxford and Cambridge?

4.18

The TV programme *That Was The Week That Was* came out of the BBC's Current Affairs Department, not Light Entertainment. The series ran for two short seasons in 1962 and 1963. It was taken off the air by the BBC in view of the imminent General Election.

4.17

The revue *Beyond the Fringe* was performed by graduates of the universities of Oxford and Cambridge

The satirical magazine *Private Eye* which began in 1961 and is still going strong.

Monty Python's Flying Circus, a popular TV programme of the 1970s in which, among other things, a Ministry of Silly Walks was established and a government minister fell through the earth's crust during a party political broadcast.

Central TV's *Spitting Image* caricatures leading political figures in puppet form.

Some writers have seen this type of comedy as **functional** for the political system (see 4.22), and others argue that the satirist tends, perhaps unknowingly, to endorse a right-wing political philosophy (see 4.23).

ACTIVITY 9

A (i) How might a satirist demonstrate the difference between the ideals of political theory and 'the human nature of the practitioners'? (4.22)

(ii) In what sense is this seen as 'functional' for the political system?

B In what ways could political satire be thought to promote 'right wing iconoclasm'? (4.23)

C (i) To what extent do you agree with either of the views expressed in 4.22 and 4.23?

(ii) Are there any other possible ways of explaining the role of political satire?

D If you were a leading politician what would be your response to being caricatured frequently in *Spitting Image*?

4.22

Comedians and satirists are playing the historic role of the Fool, who reminds us of the difference between the ideals of the theory, with its ritual and symbols – the mace, the crown, the judge's wig (stressing the impersonality of justice) – and the human nature of the practitioners.

Source: adapted from Colin Seymour-Ure, *The Political Impact of the Mass Media*, Constable, 1974

4.23

Undeniably savage and daring in some of its portrayals, *Spitting Image* is based ultimately on the same right wing iconoclasm [image breaking] as *That Was The Week That Was* and *Private Eye*, assuming everyone in the public eye to be equally suspect and open to ridicule, irrespective of creed or cause.

Source: Stephen Wagg, *Marxism Today*, February 1987

E. Reinforcing political attitudes: nation, gender and war in the popular press

This section examines the view that parts of the media perpetuate divisions within society by reinforcing stereotypical attitudes towards the sexes, different ethnic groups and the nation. The general tenor of the popular press approach in these areas was neatly encapsulated by John Sweeney (*Observer Magazine*, 7 August 1988) thus: 'We like big tits, but we don't like wogs'. These portrayals have clear implications for political parties committed to eroding these divisions. The popular press does affect public attitudes toward political issues which concern the sexes (equal opportunities legislation), the races (immigration, anti-racist programmes, conditions in the inner cities) and the nation itself (the Falklands War of 1982).

ACTIVITY 10

A Carry out your own survey of the popular press. Collect examples of stereotyping and classify them according to whether they reinforce attitudes of sex, race or nation. Which papers in particular use such stereotypes?

B Study 4.24. What implications might the nationalistic vocabulary of the popular press have for party politics in Britain?

4.24

Xenophobic headlines

HOP OFF YOU FROGS – when French lorry drivers protested against the import of British lamb (1982).

THE KRAUT – when Boris Becker was involved in a minor dispute at Wimbledon (1988).

ARGIE AND FERGIE'S SIS – when the Duchess of York's sister met an Argentine friend (1988).

Source: *The Sun Newspaper*

Specifically with regard to ethnic relations, three interrelated themes can be discerned in the popular press in the 1980s: the alleged lawlessness of English Afro-Caribbeans (data 4.25), the supposed antagonism between Caribbeans and Asians (4.26) and, thirdly, the 'racism of the anti-racists' (4.27).

ACTIVITY 11

A What are the possible effects of popular press reportage on race relations in Britain? (4.25–4.27)

B Assuming that virtually all politicians in the major political parties now formally reject racism, devise policies from both the **right** and the **left** for dealing with this kind of reportage.

4.25

BLACKS DO 60% OF LONDON MUGGINGS

Prime target for them are Asians

By VAUGHAN FREEMAN

BLACK muggers are responsible for almost 60 per cent of violent street crimes in London, a shock Government report revealed yesterday.

And a prime target for the street thugs are Asians.

The Home Office report said: "The proportion of non-white assailants for recorded offences of street robbery and other violent theft was close to 60 per cent."

The alarming statistics come in a Home Office analysis of crime statistics for the Metropolitan Police District. Covering 1982–83, the detailed dossier breaks the figures down by ethnic groups.

Source: *The Sun,* 27.9.84

The Sun used misleading headline about muggings

The Sun should not have used the firm headline "Blacks do 60 per cent of London muggings" on its story about a long, complicated and qualified Home Office report, the Press Council ruled yesterday.

The council has upheld the general complaint against the newspaper by the West Indian Standing Conference, saying the headline was too strident for an issue which called for careful, sensitive handling.

Source: *The Times,* 11.2.85

4.26

WHY THE WEST INDIANS HATE ASIANS

LESS than two weeks ago, I visited a black friend in Notting Hill Gate and found him spellbound by the eloquence of a West Indian mate from the Midlands.

The mate was saying: "Everywhere you look, even here in London, Asian shopkeepers are taking over! They're getting nearer man, there's one on your corner now.

"They don't even live in this part of London. Everyone thinks they are small family businesses with everyone helping out, but the truth is it's a plot!

"There's one big Asian cash-and-carry warehouse by the railway line near Watford and the Indian who owns that is the mastermind.

"He owns every Asian business in Britain and he employs everybody else. The illiterate ones on forged visas do the heavy work and the educated ones he puts on the tills."

Source: *The Sun,* 12.9.85

4.27

SINISTER RISE OF A NEW PHENOMENON

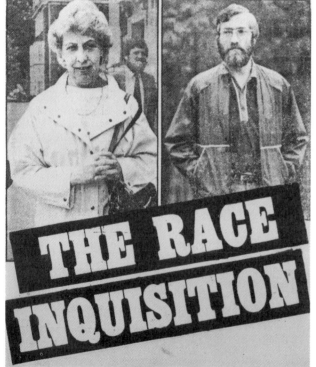

THE McCarthyite witch hunt being conducted by the race-relations fanatics of Islington's Marxist council strikes many people as funny.

'Oh, the Looney Left again,' they say. 'What will they get up to next?'

But it is no joke if you are a victim of these Labour party inquisitions. Mrs Irene Pledger an ordinary working-class Londoner, who scarcely knows what offence she is supposed to have committed, has been publicly denounced as a racist,' has been suspended from her job as a council clerk and now looks likely to lose it altogether.

In Bradford, Ray Honeyford, an honourable, experienced and much-respected headmaster has been branded with a similar charge and is fighting a desperate legal battle to save his job and his reputation.

Nowadays, on a Labour-controlled council, it is the easiest thing in the world to get rid of an enemy by denouncing him or her as a 'racist.' You are in danger of losing your job just for the crime of being 'anti-gay' or 'anti-lesbian.'

Mrs Pledger complains: 'If you're not black, gay or lesbian, you are spied on all the time. And anything you say is reported back.' Once an employee has been denounced by an informer, the chances of justice are slight, since Labour controls both the 'disciplinary hearing' and the so-called 'appeals committee.'

Mrs Pledger's barrister described the justice she received there as 'something you would expect to find in Nazi Germany or Stalin's Russia.'

Source: *Daily Mail,* 17.6.85

When, in 1982, Britain went to war with Argentina over the Falkland Islands, these ideas of gender, race and nation permeated popular press coverage of hostilities.

ACTIVITY 12

A In what ways might 'topless pin-ups' be construed as 'political'?

B It appears from their own testimony (4.29) that some journalists reporting the Falklands war for the popular press actually opposed the Government's policy on the issue. Why, then, did their newspapers support it?

4.28

The Falklands War

The *Sun* styled itself **THE PAPER THAT SUPPORTS OUR BOYS,** and flew free copies of the paper out to the task force, along with 50 two foot by six inch pictures of 'Page Three Girls'. (Young women waving off the troopships were greeted with chants of 'Get your tits out for the lads'.) The *Sun* also sponsored a Sidewinder missile, inscribed with the slogan 'Up Yours, Galtieri'. However, the *Sun* lost 40,000 readers during the campaign, while the *Daily Mirror*, whom the *Sun* at one stage accused of treason, gained 95,000. When the *Sun* ran the headline **GOTCHA** to welcome the sinking of the Argentine cruiser **General Belgrano**, many copies of the newspaper were tossed overboard by British soldiers.

4.29

A reporter's reaction

I thought it was futile and disgusting and despicable from the moment we sailed until the moment we got back. And I still feel that way. [Nevertheless], the *Star* was backing our boys,...I work for the *Star* because it's a national newspaper and it pays a lot of money. I never really gave any thought at all about what was going into the newspaper, what the editors were saying.

Source: Mick Seamark, quoted in David E Morrison and Howard Tumber
Journalists at War, Sage Publications, 1988

F. Deregulating the broadcasters – power to the people?

This section anticipates that government 'deregulation' of the broadcasting media, proposed at the time of writing, will increase the political imbalance of media commentary and general output. The mass media have always been subject to legal regulation and this regulation has in general been, overtly or obliquely, political. For instance, the Stamp Duty imposed on the pioneering newspapers of the eighteenth century was designed to make life difficult for the government's reform-minded opponents (see data 4.1). Broadcasting in Britain has been more tightly regulated than the press having, at its inception, been made the monopoly of a public corporation – the British Broadcasting Corporation. Unlike the press, the BBC, both in its radio and its television services, has always been bound by charter to be impartial in political matters. The General Strike of 1926 was the first test of this impartiality and, in this context, the BBC began as it has apparently gone on – attracting hostile reaction from both sides: for the government there was the accusation from the Conservative Sir Winston Churchill in data 4.15, but, on the other hand, no spokesperson was invited to speak for organized labour.

The BBC monopoly was finally broken by the Television Act of 1954, which established independent television, and the Sound Broadcasting Act of 1972 which legalised commercial radio – both pieces of legislation being introduced by Conservative administrations. Now, in the late 1980s, another Conservative Government has produced a White Paper, *Broadcasting in the '90s: Competition, Choice and Quality*, in which it proposes what is widely referred to as a 'deregulation' of British broadcasting (see data 4.30). Some see these proposals as the beginning of the end for 'public service broadcasting'. The Government, however, promises in the White Paper that the BBC 'will continue as the cornerstone of public service broadcasting' and has approved the continuation, for now, of the licence fee.

ACTIVITY 13

A   In what ways is it proposed that the broadcasting media will be deregulated? (4.30)

B   What is meant by the term 'public service broadcasting'?

C   Drawing on data 4.31–4.33 construct a **defence** of public service broadcasting **and** an **attack** on it from
   (i)   a Conservative perspective
   (ii) a Labour standpoint.

4.30

The Government White Paper

The White Paper promises a considerable extension of the principle of consumer sovereignty: on the cover is a hand holding a remote control panel labelled 'Choice Quality', and, on page 1, is the assertion: 'The Government places the viewer and listener at the centre of broadcasting policy'. To this end, the Government proposes: a fifth and sixth television channel; the introduction of cable and satellite broadcasting services; an Independent Television Commission to oversee all commercial television, replacing, and with 'a lighter touch' than, the existing Independent Broadcasting Authority; and a Broadcasting Standards Council to 'reinforce standards on taste and decency and the portrayal of sex and violence'.

Source: adapted from *Broadcasting in the '90s*, HMSO

4.31

...to give the public what it wants is a misleading phrase... it has the appearance of an appeal to democratic principle, but the appearance is deceptive. It is in fact patronising and arrogant, in that it claims to know what the public is but defines it as no more than the mass audience, and it claims to know what it wants, but limits its choice to the average of experience.

Source: *Pilkington Report*, 1962

4.32

State broadcasting

...in most countries, including Britain, broadcasting was seen as a legitimate extension of the national state. The state determined what people could or could not see, what constituted fairness in news, and what was 'good' as opposed to 'bad' culture. Overseen by the state, broadcasters offered a mass, standardised service... The tradition was essentially social democratic. Broadcasting was seen as something to be rationally planned and directed downwards to improve the populace.

This tradition is now breaking down. The number of channels have brought new owners and new commercial interests in many countries. Italy was the first, with its dramatic deregulation of broadcasting in the mid-1970s... In France and Spain socialist governments have used deregulation to give new channels to their political allies, just as the British government is using it to tip the political scales to the right.

Source: Geoff Mulgan, *Marxism Today*, April 1989

4.33

The future

ITV's advertising monopoly has of course always been unpopular with the advertisers, who claim they have been over-charged... Part of the advertising lobby's complaint is that ITV's monopoly has created an environment in which trade unionism has thrived... The Government is naturally sympathetic to the advertisers' call for greater competition... The overall result (of the White Paper proposals) will be a reduction in permanently employed staff to a tiny number in commissioning, administration, finance and transmission. Production will be almost entirely casualised... At present, TV's share of advertising revenue is divided between 15 regional ITV companies and Channel 4. By the start of 1993, it will be fought over by two national services on Channels 4 and 5, an indeterminate number of regional operators on Channel 3, an indeterminate number of local channels on cable and MVDS (microwave), plus 21 channels beamed down from satellite. The cost-cutting which must result cannot help but feed through into production budgets. It will lead to even heavier reliance on familiar, cheap production formulae: repeats, and studio-based talk-shows, game-shows, and soap-operas... Open-ended or high-risk programmes, such as investigative documentary or current affairs productions will be axed.

Source: adapted from Martin Spence, 'Behind the News: The White Paper on Broadcasting' *Capital and Class*, No 38, 1989

G. What better way?

As we have seen, the relationship between politics and the media has attracted strong and widespread criticism. Such criticism has been reflected in a large number of proposals for reform. This final section considers the alternative ways of organising mass media in a modern society which might correct existing political imbalances.

ACTIVITY 14

A   Most of the popular newspapers support the Conservatives (data 4.11). Examine the difficulties facing those who might try, in a free market, to set up a popular newspaper which took a socialist stance.

B   What is meant by 'greater professionalism among journalists', and in what way could it change the media politically? (4.34)

C   Present a case for and against a right to reply for those criticised by the media.

D   There already is an Independent Broadcasting Authority. Why isn't there an Independent Press Authority? (4.34)

E   Some people say the media need democratising. Others say the media already are democratic. Examine different ways in which the media might be, or might be made, democratic.

F   What criteria might a National Printing Corporation (4.34) employ in allocating print facilities?

G   Present cases for and against the nationalisation of press and broadcasting facilities.

4.34

Approaches to media reform

Liberal Market Approaches These are various versions of the free market philosophy, opposed to state intervention, but not always from a right wing position. Some people argue that such things as the promotion of greater professionalism among journalists, the right of reply, the providing of well constructed counter argument by leftist organisations (like trade unions) who are often criticised by the media, and the utilising of cost saving technology by such groups, make possible a counterbalancing of the current right wing dominance of the media.

Public Service Approaches These include the proposing of an Independent Press Authority (modelled on the IBA), a press ombudsman, a strengthened Press Council, legal safeguards against pressure by proprietors on editors, and a democratisation of trusteeship, so that, for example, the governors of the BBC would include elected representatives of trade unions and other bodies.

Radical Market Approaches Which encompass anti-monopoly legislation, the establishment of a National Printing Corporation and a Media Enterprise Board which would broaden the access to capital of people who, say, wanted to start a newspaper.

Socialist Approaches Which argue for the nationalising of all press and broadcasting facilities. Some on the political left suggest that, once this was done, editorial control could be exercised at the respective newspapers and broadcasting channels by political parties, while the actual means of media production would be run by consortia of relevant trade unionists, TUC officials and government appointees.

Source: James Curran, 'The different approaches to media reform', in J Curran, J Ecclestone, G Oakley and A Richardson (eds), *Bending Reality*, Pluto Press, 1986 pp 89–135

Further reading

Baistow, Tom, *Fourth Rate Estate: An Anatomy of Fleet Street*, Comedia, 1985
Curran, James *et al* (ed), *Bending Reality*, Pluto Press, 1986
Curran, James & Seaton, Jean, *Power Without Responsibility*: The Press and Broadcasting in Britain, Methuen, 1985
Glasgow University Media Group, *Really Bad News*, Readers & Writers, 1982
Negrine, Ralph, *Politics and the Mass Media in Britain*, Routledge, 1989
Tunstall, Jeremy, *The Media in Britain*, Constable, 1983
Whale, John, *The Politics of the Media*, Fontana/Collins, 1977

UNIT 5   Public Opinion

'The great objective of any government is to increase its standing with the electorate.' (J.P. Mackintosh, *The British Cabinet*)

'Public opinion is simply one more problem that demands skilful management.' (R.J. Barnet, *Roots of War*)

Introduction

These accounts of the role of public opinion in the political process appear to contradict one another. The first suggests that public opinion controls political leaders; the second indicates that political leaders attempt to manipulate public opinion. This unit is intended to clarify whether these statements are contradictory. If this is the case; then which one is accurate? If they are compatible, then how could this be explained? These and other questions can only be solved by first defining what we mean when we talk about 'public opinion'.

A. Defining public opinion

Public opinion is sometimes described as the attitude held by most people on any particular issue. But, on controversial issues, there is no generally agreed public opinion. Indeed, pressure groups, parties and individuals can be bitterly divided. On these issues, it is useful to see the general public as a series of 'little publics'. They can be united or divided depending on the issue. Public opinion can be defined by looking at three characteristics.

Political scientists measure the **direction** of opinions by placing them on a scale from 'left' to 'right' (5.1). Opinions can vary in **intensity** as well as direction. A hunt saboteur is likely to hold very stong opinions. By comparison, most people do not hold such strong opinions on the EEC. We can also measure opinion by its **stability**. Opinions change through time. For example, most people no longer believe that the earth is flat.

ACTIVITY 1

For each of the statements below ask yourself (or a class colleague) how you would answer questions A to E. Give reasons for each answer.

Questions

A   Do you agree very stongly/quite strongly, disagree very strongly/quite strongly, or are you unsure about this issue?

B   Do the parties agree or disagree over this issue?

C   If they disagree, how do they differ and why?

D   Would you describe your opinion on this issue as being on the 'left', the 'right' or neither?

E   Is the issue short-term or long-term?

Statements

1   The police should prosecute people for cruelty to animals.

2   We should bring back the death penalty.

3   Citizens should have the right to see the contents of all government files containing their personal details.

4   Student grants should be replaced by student loans.

ACTIVITY 2
With the help of data 5.1 and 5.2, suggest why the measurement of public opinion is not a straightforward matter. Support your answer with examples.

'Grayson is a liberal in social matters, a conservative in economic matters and a homicidal psychopath in political matters.'

5.2

Political Spectrum

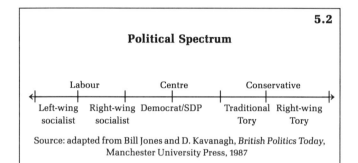

Source: adapted from Bill Jones and D. Kavanagh, *British Politics Today*, Manchester University Press, 1987

B. Socialisation and public opinion

Everyone needs to make sense of the world beyond their experience. Whether an opinion concerns nuclear deterrence, the death penalty or support for the poor, we often form judgements which are based on 'second hand' information. The process of acquiring political attitudes over the years is known as **political socialisation**.

The family is thought to have a major influence on the opinions we hold. We don't simply absorb a set of beliefs and attitudes from family life. Many people hold different views from those of their parents. This is because as children grow older, they get their information from other sources such as school, college, work and television.

At school, pupils learn something about Parliament, democracy and other basic values of our political system. There are some courses which deal exclusively with politics and government. Surveys suggest that students are more influenced by the opinions of their friends than of their teachers.

There are plenty of other groups who seek to influence our opinion. Pressure groups, political parties and politicians all compete for public support. Whilst these groups play a significant role, other factors may also influence our political opinions. Whether we are young or old, middle or working class, and whether we live in the North or South all influence our political outlook.

ACTIVITY 3

Look at the pictures and personal details in data 5.4.

A How might each individual *typically* be expected to vote in an election?

B Do the figures in the tables (data 5.3) support your guess? Explain your answer.

C Compare the way that each class, age group and region votes with the national average (given in the right hand column of each table). Which characteristic is the best indicator of how someone will vote?

5.3

Voting by class and age (per cent)

| | CLASS | | AGE | | | | |
	MIDDLE	WORKING	18–24	25–34	35–54	55+	ALL
Total	43	57	14	19	33	34	100
Con.	54	35	37	39	45	46	43
Lab.	18	42	40	33	29	31	32
Alln.	26	22	21	25	24	21	23

Voting by region (per cent)

	South	England Midlands	North	Wales	Scotland	U.K.
Con.	52	48	37	30	24	43
Lab.	21	30	42	45	42	32
Alln.	27	22	21	18	19	23

Source: adapted from D. Butler & D. Kavanagh, *The British General Election of 1987*, Macmillon, 1988, pp 275 & 284

5.4

Penelope lives in Surrey and belongs to the middle class. She is 35 years old.

Kelvin lives in Central Scotland and belongs to the working class. He is 23.

James lives in Hertfordshire and belongs to the middle class. He is 40 years old.

Joan lives in Yorkshire and belongs to the working class. She is 46 years old.

C. The mass media and public opinion

The mass media is a catch-all phrase which includes television, newspapers, radio, books and magazines. Because most people depend on the media for political information, its accuracy is fundamental to democracy. The central issue is whether it shapes or reflects public opinion. Perhaps it does both.

Newspapers

One major difference between broadcasters and the press is that broadcasters are legally bound to be unbiased while newspapers are not. Newspapers can be divided into two groups. The **tabloids** are generally more interested in gossip and sport. They tend to openly support political parties. In the run-up to the 1987 election the 'soar away' *Sun* published a 'Special Nightmare Issue – Life under the Socialists'. The *Mirror* tends to support Labour and during the same campaign told its readers 'Thousands of Disabled People Face Death because of Benefit Cuts'.

Broad-sheet papers, like the *Times* and the *Guardian*, attempt a more serious coverage of events. The *Guardian* generally supports the centre parties and Labour, while the *Times* and *Telegraph* generally support the Conservatives.

A survey conducted after the 1987 election suggested that readers believed that newspaper coverage had more influence on their attitudes to parties than posters and leaflets. They thought that they were about as reliable as election broadcasts and less reliable than television. Data 5.6 suggests that there is a close match between the bias of newspapers and the way their readers vote. It is probably fair to say that the immediate effect of newspapers on public opinion is largely confined to reinforcing existing loyalties.

ACTIVITY 4

A   Having read the headlines (5.7) and data 5.6 rearrange the daily newspapers into three groups, Conservative papers, Labour papers and those in the centre.

B   From your own reading, rearrange the papers on a political scale from 'left' to 'right'. This can be done as a class exercise.

C   What does the ownership of each paper tell you about the party it supports? (5.5)

D   Using data 5.5, what is the daily circulation of the Conservative press and the Labour press?

5.5

National daily newspapers, 1987

PAPER	CHAIRMAN	CIRCULATION
Daily Telegraph	Lord Hartwell	1,147,000
The Times	R. Murdoch	442,000
Independent	Lord Sieff	293,000
Guardian	P. Gibbings	494,000
Sun	R. Murdoch	3,993,000
Daily Mail	Viscount Rothermere	1,759,000
Daily Express	D. Stevens	1,697,000
Today	R. Murdoch	307,000
Daily Mirror	R. Maxwell	3,123,000

Source: Butler and Kavanagh, *op. cit.*, p. 165–6

5.6

Party supported by newspaper readers and perceptions of bias, 1987

Daily newspaper	PARTY SUPPORTED BY READERS			READERS' PERCEPTIONS OF PAPER'S BIAS			
	Con. %	Lab. %	Alln. %	Con. %	Lab. %	Alln. %	Don't know %
Daily Telegraph	80	5	10	85	0	3	12
The Times	55	12	27	61	0	33	6
Independent	34	34	27	12	6	20	62
Guardian	22	54	19	13	30	43	14
Sun	41	31	19	63	12	7	18
Daily Mail	60	13	19	78	2	5	15
Daily Express	70	9	18	87	0	4	9
Today	43	17	40	11	4	18	67
Daily Mirror	20	55	21	2	84	8	6

Source: Butler and Kavanagh, *op. cit.*, p.187

5.7

Television

This section examines the relationship between television broadcasting and public opinion. Does television lead opinion or is it led by it? Who has the power of persuasion, broadcasters or their audience? Broadcasters tell us what everyone else is thinking and to that extent they reinforce what society sees as 'normal'.

Unlike newspapers, television documentaries and news programmes have a legal duty to be impartial. Although broadcasters see themselves as neutral, they have been criticised for being biased by politicians ranging from Tony Benn to Norman Tebbit. Bias could take various forms. For example, more time could be given to one side of the argument than another. In 1986, the Alliance parties issued a High Court writ against the BBC for giving them too little air-time. A few months before the 1987 General Election, Norman Tebbit attacked the BBC's coverage of the air raid on Libya by American jets based in the UK. He accused the BBC of bias against Mrs Thatcher in the form of 'slanted reporting' and an uncritical airing of 'Libyan propaganda'. Even though Mr Tebbit believes that the BBC is sympathetic to Labour and Mr Benn thinks it favours the Conservatives, they both seem to agree that broadcasters can influence public opinion. Why else would they complain when they feel that their opponents are receiving more favourable coverage?

ACTIVITY 5

A   Study data 5.8–5.10. Is it possible to ensure impartiality in television coverage? If not, why not?

B   What does data 5.11 tell you about the source of news for most people? What change occurred over the six-year period?

C   Looking at data 5.12, would you say that the public thinks television is politically biased?

D   Which channel is thought to be most biased and which party is it thought to favour?

E   You are a television journalist accused by a political party of being biased against it. Prepare a defence to the accusation.

5.8

Tebbit commissions fresh report on BBC

'I suggest you get your eyes tested, you just can't get the picture straight.'

5.9

Impartiality 1

Contrary to the claims, conventions, and culture of television journalism, the news is not a neutral product. Bulletins show a systematic presentation of a particular and narrow view. Alternatives to this dominent view have little chance of surfacing in a meaningful way.

Source: adapted from The Glasgow Media Group, *Bad News*, RKP, 1976

5.11

Sources of most world news

	1981	1982	1983	1984	1985	1986
Television	53	58	60	62	62	65
Radio	11	12	10	13	14	10
Newspapers	34	27	28	23	23	23

Source: *Attitudes to Broadcasting in 1986*, IBA

5.10

Impartiality 2

Broadcasters too often forget that to represent management at their desks, apparently the calm and collected representatives of order, and to represent shop stewards and picket lines stopping production, apparently the agents of disruption, gives a false picture of what strikes are about.

Broadcasters are operating within a system of parliamentary democracy and must share its assumptions. They should not be expected to give equal weight or to show an impartiality which is not due to those who seek to destroy it by violent, unparliamentary or illegal means.

Broadcasters must take account, not just of the whole range of views on an issue, but also of the weight of opinion which holds these views. Their duty to let the public hear various voices does not oblige them to give more weight or coverage to opinions which are not widely held. While it is right that the accepted orthodoxies should be challenged, equally it is essential that the established views should be fully and clearly put and that the status and implications of the challenge should be made clear.

The range of views and the weight of opinion are constantly changing. What may be an acceptable and justifiable approach to an issue at any one time will not necessarily remain so for all time.

Source: *The Annan Report*, 1977

5.12

Viewers' beliefs about political bias, 1986

	ITV	BBC1	BBC2	Ch.4
Channel does not favour any party	73	62	67	64
Channel favours a particular party	11	24	12	8
Don't know	16	14	21	28
Which party favoured?				
Conservative	4	18	10	1
Labour	6	5	2	5
Lib/SDP Alliance	—	—	—	—

Source: IBA *op. cit.*

D. Pressure groups and public opinion

What role do pressure groups play? Do they reflect public opinion? Do they influence public opinion? Or is the truth somewhere between? Pressure groups differ from parties because they usually have limited objectives and seldom field candidates in elections. **Protective groups** such as business, the unions and professional organisations seek to protect their own interests. For example, the CBI or the TUC concentrate on influencing economic policy. **Promotional groups**, on the other hand, usually support a cause which does not directly or only benefit their members. Organisations such as Oxfam, Greenpeace or the RSPCA come into this category.

Joining a pressure group is one way of influencing government decisions between elections. In this sense, pressure groups are an expression of public opinion. Before proposing legislation, governments consult various 'interested parties' and an enormous range of groups submit evidence to Ministers, their civil servants and to MPs. Some pressure groups rely more than others on public opinion for support.

In the event of failure to influence government successfully, pressure groups can apply pressure by attempting to mobilise mass public opinion. Publicity campaigns compete for public support in the media. Employers may be in dispute with unions or environmentalists with polluters and so on.

If a publicity campaign does not work, protective groups can exert economic pressure. Unions can strike, and companies can stop production or close factories. The danger of pressure group politics is that the wealthier groups can present their case more effectively.

ACTIVITY 6

A Which of the posters in data 5.14 do you think is most effective in putting its case? Say why.

B Rearrange the posters into two types
   (i) promotional groups and
   (ii) protective groups.

C Choose **one** of the pressure groups represented in 5.14.
   (i) Write a letter to your local paper supporting its campaign.
   (ii) Write a reply from the opposite point of view.

D With reference to 5.13 and 5.14 name three general factors which determine whether a pressure group succeeds.

5.13

CPAG: the inside story

From 1965 onwards, CPAG had reasonably good coverage in The Guardian, but achieving equally good exposure in The Times was important as polls showed that this paper was more commonly read by Tory MPs and senior civil servants. Slowly, coverage was also extended to the Financial Times, and from there to the popular papers. For a considerable period of time both the Daily Mirror and the Sun gave more than fair coverage to CPAG's news stories. Where the Group's coverage was poor, and remained weak, was amongst the Daily Mail/Daily Express readership.

The up-market programmes like Panorama would occasionally give the Group's campaigns consideration. There was similarly good coverage on the early-morning breakfast programmes and, most important of all, the Jimmy Young Show. A working relationship was quickly established with what was known as 'The JY Prog'.

The media coverage had a number of important dynamic consequences. As Professor Mackenzie suggests, politicians' response to the Group was increased because of the coverage it was able to obtain, which MPs took as a sign of the Group's importance. The coverage had a more immediate impact on ministers. Early on, it became very clear that while detailed and often prolonged correspondence with a department was important in trying to corner a minister, because of the size of his post not all letters were read as carefully as they should be. One way of getting the Group's correspondence onto the top of the pile and read by ministers was to ensure publicity for the letters in the media. Partly through natural interest, but also the need for protection when facing the Commons or the media itself, ministers would then request an internal briefing (further information on the subject from civil servants in their department), thereby getting the department's attention into the issue being raised by the Group.

Source: Frank Field, *Poverty and Politics*, Heinemann Educational Books, London, 1982

5.14

E. Parties and public opinion

In some ways, political parties are like pressure groups. They are voluntary organisations which unite for common political purposes. They differ from pressure groups because they field candidates for office and, if they win enough seats in the House of Commons, they form a government. Each party consists of supporters with varying degrees of commitment. At the centre, there are the full time officers, like party leader. In the constituencies, each party has a number of dedicated activists who raise funds, recruit members, select parliamentary candidates and deliver election addresses. Then there are the ordinary members who may help in election campaigns but are usually inactive.

Outside the party organisation, each party has supporters who vote at election times. They too vary in their support for the party. There are the strong supporters who 'always have and always will' turn out for their party on election day. There is a second group of voters who will usually support their party but who are open to persuasion by other parties. There are also a large number of 'floating' voters who are undecided on which party to vote for. Both a party's membership, and its support at elections, are expressions of **organised public opinion**.

Parties do not just announce what they stand for and wait to see how voters respond. They actively seek to influence public opinion in two ways. Firstly, they try to persuade people of opposing views to vote for them. Secondly, they draw attention to issues which they think will win them votes. In this way they are creating public opinion because they focus on issues which people may not have considered before.

Generally, the main parties are built upon a coalition of interests. For example, the Labour Party is largely supported by the unions whilst the Conservative Party is supported by business. This explains why the policies of each party reflect the interests of these groups. It could be argued that parties and pressure groups complement one another. Parties represent geographical constituencies and pressure groups represent particular interests. Some pressure groups seek to work through parties: CND, for example, is active within the Labour Party.

ACTIVITY 7
Study data 5.15–5.18

A Which of the posters do you think carries the most convincing slogan, and why?
B Which of the posters do you think would have had the most influence on public opinion as a whole and why?
C Which groups' interests are served by each poster? Say why.
D Do the posters try to appeal to peoples' feelings, or their rational interests, or both?

Source: Conservative Party, 1987

5.16

WE HAVE OUTLAWED SECONDARY PICKETING AND THE VIOLENCE THAT GOES WITH IT.

Labour would bring back secondary picketing.

THE BASIC RATE OF INCOME TAX IS DOWN TO ITS LOWEST FOR NEARLY 50 YEARS.

Labour would put it up again.

Source: *Conservative Party*, 1987

5.17

UNDER THE TORIES YOUR CHILD'S EDUCATION COULD DEPEND ON JUST ONE BOOK, YOUR CHEQUE BOOK.

IN BRITAIN THE POOR HAVE GOT POORER AND THE RICH HAVE GOT. . . WELL, THEY'VE GOT THE CONSERVATIVES.

Source: *Labour Party*, 1987

5.18

THE CONSERVATIVE MANIFESTO DOESN'T SAY ANYTHING ABOUT REDUCING UNEMPLOYMENT.

IT DOESN'T SAY ANYTHING ABOUT IMPROVING THE HEALTH SERVICE.

IT DOESN'T SAY ANYTHING ABOUT INVESTING IN EDUCATION.

IT DOESN'T SAY ANYTHING ABOUT BUILDING MORE HOUSES.

IT SAYS A LOT ABOUT THE CONSERVATIVES.

"IF UNEMPLOYMENT IS NOT BELOW THREE MILLION IN FIVE YEARS, THEN I'M NOT WORTH RE-ELECTING."

Norman Tebbit, 1983

No wonder they've called the election a year early.

Source: *Labour Party*, 1987

F. Government and public opinion

A government is said to be 'democratic' because it responds to public opinion – the more responsive, the more democratic it is. However the last time a party won office with more than 50% of votes cast was in 1935! Since then, one government was formed with as little as 38% of the vote. As general elections have become three-cornered contests, it has become possible to win office with the support of fewer than 30% of registered electors – a comparatively narrow section of the public.

Once in office, a party should strictly speaking, represent public opinion as a whole. There is no difficulty when the public generally agrees, for example, that steps need to be introduced to stem a rise in crime. The problem comes when the issue is controversial. The government usually has a view but may not be supported by the whole electorate. Although governments seek to maximise their support, they may sometimes feel it is necessary to impose difficult decisions on certain groups. When doing this they have to handle public opinion very carefully, otherwise they risk defeat at the next election. Their top priority is to keep the support of those sections of the electorate which voted them into power.

Public opinion polls inform government of how the electorate is reacting to its policies. By-elections and local elections also help governments to gauge public feelings. When it is unsure of public opinion, it can 'test the water' by leaking its plans.

Although public reactions to the government restrict what it can do, it is uniquely placed to guide public opinion. A government can put its case at press conferences and in TV interviews. It can launch advertising campaigns to promote particular objectives. Some government campaigns promote policies which are generally supported whilst others are more controversial.

ACTIVITY 8

A   Look at the government adverts (5.20) and indicate which ones represent the public as a whole.

B   Which of these adverts might be seen as controversial and why?

C   Which advert is the most eye-catching and puts its message across most effectively? Say why.

D   After reading data 5.19, explain what 'kite-flying' refers to.

E   What are the advantages and disavantages of the 'lobby system' mentioned in data 5.19?

F   It is said that Mrs Thatcher is successful in manipulating public opinion through the media. In what way does data 5.21 illustrate this ability?

5.19

Lawsongate: an exercise in political kite-flying

Mr Lawson turned immediately to the pensioners. He was reminded that most OAPs would soon have to pay for eye tests and dental check-ups: did that set a pattern?

'The problem with pensioners,' replies the Chancellor, 'is that there is a minority who do have difficulty in making ends meet.'

'A minority?'

'Yes, a tiny minority. Pensioners as a whole are doing very much better than ever before, because more and more have occupational pensions, more and more have Serps on top of that basic pension, and more and more have savings bringing a real return. Unlike when inflation was high, the income of pensioners has been rising faster on average than the increase of the waged.'

What were the implications of this new class of wealthy pensioners for the benefits system?

'We have got to see in the evolution of the social security system whether we can do better targeting there, so we can help that minority of pensioners who have genuine difficulty in making ends meet.'

Pens set racing

It was that phrase — 'evolution of the social security system' — and that word — 'targeting' — which sent pens racing across notebooks. None of us got the impression that Mr Lawson was merely talking about a new payment on top of existing allowances.

As with child benefit, it sounded as though what he had in mind was a fundamental 'restructuring' — switching resources from universal

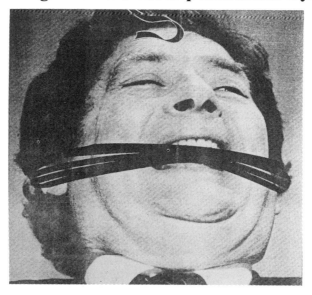

benefits which go to everyone, however rich, and putting money instead into means-tested payments, targeted on the poorest.

Indeed, the very next question reflected that conviction. The Chancellor was asked whether, in the light of that week's Commons rebellion over charges for dental and eye tests, such a change would require him 'to educate more of your backbenchers to that view?'

Mr Lawson agreed, but added that that particular rebellion had 'comprised people who had very different motivations'.

How, then, might these changes in the social security system come about?

'There are no study groups at the moment,' he replied, 'but in

my opinion that is the way we are likely to go.

'Of course, the state pension is regularly uprated. It is a pledged benefit. Child benefit was not pledged. You can find all these benefits and whether they are pledged or not in Parliamentary answers.'

Again, there seemed to be no mistaking the Chancellor's meaning. Not content with hinting at a restructuring of pensioners' benefits, he was now inviting us to look up the very list which would show which payments he was pledged to uprate, and which he wasn't. Among those 'unpledged' benefits was the pensioners' £10 Christmas bonus.

AT 11a.m. Mr Lawson thanked

us for coming and left. He seemed well satisfied with the way things had gone (indeed, he remarked at one point: 'I always enjoy meeting you all' — not a sentiment he would be likely to express today).

At this point, his Press adviser, John Gieve, steps into the story. Mr Gieve — a newcomer to his job — announced that the Chancellor's remarks had been 'on the record'.

Standing outside in Downing Street, the Press corps digested this stunning news. As one journalist later put it: 'It was obvious to us it was a major story — on the record, it was a cosmic story.'

Within an hour, Mr Gieve had rung all 10 journalists to apologise and say that the Chancellor's remarks were actually non-attributable. But by then, the damage was done. Newsdesks had been alerted to this rare example of open government, and word was already seeping out around Whitehall.

Lobby discredited

THE likelihood is that 'Lawsongate' — like the Westland affair — will now expire for lack of fresh information. The Cabinet has turned down Labour's request for a debate. The earliest the matter could now be debated is December, by which time the issue will be dead.

But it will not be forgotten. It has further discredited the lobby system, shining a bright light on the furtive system of hints and innuendo by which the Government floats stories in the Press.

Source: *Observer*, 13.11.88

5.20

5.21

Mrs Thatcher with multi-millionaire Charles Forte at the official
opening of his new motorway services on the M25 in 1987

G. Elections, referenda and public opinion

So far, we have looked at a variety of **influences** on public opinion. In the next two sections we turn our attention to ways that public opinion is **measured**. Elections are the most important test of public opinion. The votes cast for each party represent a '*snapshot*' of public opinion. Of course, not everyone is able to cast a vote – under 18 year olds, the Royal family, Peers of the Realm, the certifiably insane and prison inmates are not eligible. Of the remaining population only people listed on the electoral register can vote. In 1987 75% of registered electors cast their votes, representing only 57% of the population.

There are four main types of election: local council elections, Euro-elections, by-elections and general elections. At each of these there are different factors which may affect voting choices. For example, the same voter is being asked to consider different issues in a local election compared with a European election.

By-elections are unique because voters are not usually being asked to choose a government. In rare cases, a by-election can topple a government with a 'knife-edge' majority but usually they are seen as 'litmus tests' of public opinion between general elections. Supposing that a government is defeated at a general election after a small swing of opinion, the new government could introduce radical changes of direction.

Public opinion can be directly consulted over specific issues during a government's term of office. This is called a referendum. Referenda have decided whether Britain should remain in the EEC (1975) and whether Scotland and Wales should have elected assemblies (1979).

ACTIVITY 9

A   Did the public's policy preferences (5.22) reflect the way that they voted?

B   Looking at data 5.22, which policies would you say were most important to Conservative voters? And which were least important?

C   Did people's leadership preferences (5.22) reflect the way they voted?

D   Looking at data 5.23, which by-election went against the national trend? Suggest why this might have happened.

E   After reading data 5.24, argue a case either for or against the more frequent use of referenda to decide specific issues.

5.22

The 1987 General Election

	CON. (%)	LAB. (%)	ALLN. (%)	DON'T KNOW/ /OTHER (%)
Taking everything into account, which party has the best policies?	37	27	18	19
Which party has the best policies to deal with:				
Inflation & prices	54	23	11	12
Unemployment	30	41	16	13
Defence	54	21	15	11
The NHS	25	44	19	12
Education	31	38	20	12
Law and order	42	27	14	17
And which party has the best leaders?	46	27	14	12
1987 election result	43	32	23	—

Source: D. Butler and D. Kavanagh, *op. cit.*

5.23

By-elections

	STANDING IN NATIONAL OPINION POLLS	BY-ELECTION RESULT (% OF VOTES CAST)
Fulham: '86		
Conservative	34	35
Labour	36	44
Alliance	29	19
Greenwich: '87		
Conservative	41	11
Labour	34	34
Alliance	21	53

Source: MORI

5.24

Referenda results

1975 – 73% of electors voted on whether the UK should stay in the European Community. Of these, 65% voted 'yes' to continued membership.

1979 – 64% of electors in Scotland voted on whether power should be devolved to a separate Scottish Assembly. Although a majority (52%) of voters said 'yes', they only amounted to 33% of the electorate and fell short of the 40% minimum required.

1979 – 59% of Welsh electors turned out to decide whether power should be devolved to Wales. A majority of voters said 'no'.

H. Public opinion polls

The mass media, pressure groups, parties and governments are all interested in public opinion. Do they enjoy public support? How strongly do people feel about each issue? Is public opinion united or divided and is it moving towards one side of the argument or the other? In the past, politicians relied on a 'hunch', on what the press were saying or on the atmosphere in the House of Commons. Since 1945 more scientific methods of measuring public opinion have been developed. Public opinion polls set out to discover what the public is thinking by interviewing a small **sample** of the electorate.

Supporters of opinion polls argue that they express public concern or support between elections. They also act as a balance against some pressure groups because they report the feelings of the whole public, not just the more vocal groups. With a few exceptions, polls have accurately predicted the results of general elections. They work within a 4% margin of error so when an election result looks close, they cannot be relied upon. Polls are used by those advising parties on how to plan their election campaigns.

On the other hand they can be inaccurate if the sample does not represent the whole electorate or if the researchers ask leading questions.

Polls can have important political effects. If they show one party trailing far behind, many of its supporters may decide that their vote is wasted. They may decide not to vote or to cast their vote **tactically**. For example, if your favourite party has no hope in your constituency, would you switch to your second choice as a way of keeping out your least preferred party?

ACTIVITY 10

A Suppose that the Prime Minister had asked you to advise on whether it would be safe to announce a general election. Using the figure and the chart in data 5.25 5.26 what would your advice have been:
  (i)   in July 1983?
  (ii) in July 1984?
  (iii) in April 1987?
B Bearing in mind data 5.27–5.28, explain to the PM why your advice is not foolproof.
C Look at data 5.25. What effect did the Alliance by-election victories have on their national standing during the weeks immediately after?
D Do your conclusions suggest that there is a 'bandwagon effect'?

5.25

Party support 1983–87

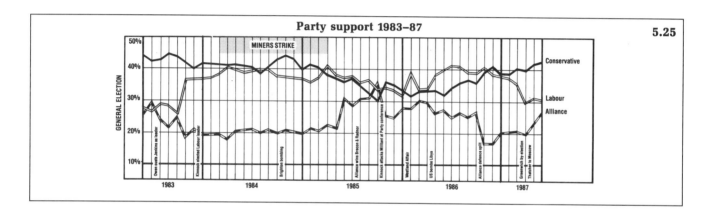

5.26

Votes and seats

% VOTING		SEATS IN PARLIAMENT		
CON.	LAB.	CON.	LAB.	OTHER
39	40	299	315	36
40	30	348	244	58
43	28	389	211	50

5.27

The bandwagon effect

Scholars have suggested that there may be a 'bandwagon effect'. People often compare their views to the dominant public opinion before speaking out. Elizabeth Noelle-Neumann (Public Opinion quarterly, vol 41) argues that there exists a 'spiral process which prompts...individuals to perceive the changes in opinion and to follow suit...'

Source: adapted from M. Cummings and D. Wise, Democracy under Pressure, HBJ, 1985

5.28

Disadvantages of polls

They prove nothing...Morally speaking, opinion polls are always an embarrassment. Touted as representing public opinion, they in fact represent only private or mass opinion: opinion taken in the dark of the doorway rather than in the open light of the forum; opinion that chokes off the opportunity to hear out arguments pro and con, to consult a neighbour, to read up, to ask a question, to answer back; opinion so half-hearted it is hard to take seriously.

Source: Conrad Jameson, 'Who needs polls?', New Statesman, 6 February, 1981, pp. 13–14

I. Conclusion

This unit opened with two apparently contradictory statements. The first implied that politicians are controlled by public opinion and the second suggested that they are able to manipulate public opinion. Bearing in mind the data in this unit, you will probably agree that both statements are true. Governments, political parties and pressure groups all claim to represent public opinion, but they also claim to 'educate' the public.

Public opinion is shaped by the process of political socialisation. The family, peer groups, education and the media all play a part in this process. Pressure groups, political parties and governments compete for public support. In so doing, they often seek to persuade public opinion to their way of thinking. They may well make use of some of the agents of political socialisation to achieve this end.

Public opinion has become increasingly important in British politics. Elections and opinion polls can be used to measure it, although they are not always completely accurate. Critics of the role of public opinion feel that the public are not sufficiently interested and do not have all the information necessary to reach a decision. Some even argue that the public can be convinced by whoever hires the most effective advertising agency. Supporters of public participation say that a democracy is only healthy when there is constant competition between various groups. Political scientists describe such a society as pluralist. Pluralism means that power is shared by many (plural) groups appealing to politicians and the public for their support.

Further reading

E. Dreyer & W. Rosenbaum, *Political Opinion and Electoral Behaviour*
G. Heald & R.J. Wybrow, *The Gallup Survey of Great Britain*, Croom Helm, 1986
R. Waller, *Moulding Public Opinion*, Croom Helm, 1987
Public Opinion Quarterly
Contemporary Record

UNIT 6 Political Parties

Where does power lie within British political parties? Are the power structures of the Labour and Conservative parties basically the same? These questions will be examined in the context of the relationship between the party in Parliament and the mass party outside.

Introduction

Political parties are the backbone of the modern political system in Britain and perform essential functions – to seek political power or influence those in power and to provide a main avenue of political recruitment. Both the Labour and Conservative parties have developed organisational structures to perform these functions. The aim of this unit is to compare the structures of the two major parties and identify the balance of power between parliamentary and mass organisations within each. R. T. McKenzie's argument – that the power structures of the two main parties are fundamentally the same – can be used as a starting point.

A. McKenzie's thesis

ACTIVITY 1
Read data 6.1

A According to McKenzie, what governs the distribution of power within British political parties?

B Who will exercise effective decision-making power?

C Which group inside the party will the leaders most rely on?

D What importance does McKenzie give to the extra-parliamentary party?

E What conclusion does McKenzie draw in this extract?

6.1

The McKenzie thesis

The distribution of power within British political parties is primarily a function of cabinet government and the British parliamentary system. So long as the parties accept this system of government effective decision-making authority will reside with the leadership groups thrown up by the parliamentary parties (of whom much the most important individual is the party leader); and they will exercise this authority so long as they retain the confidence of their respective parliamentary parties. The views of their organised supporters outside parliament must inevitably be taken into account by the party leadership because of the importance of the role these supporters play in selecting candidates, raising funds, and promoting the cause of the party during elections. But, whatever the role granted in theory to the extra-parliamentary wings of the parties, in practice final authority rests in both parties with the parliamentary party and its leadership. In this fundamental respect the distribution of power within the two main major parties is the same.

Source: R. T. McKenzie, *British Political Parties*, Mercury Books, 1963, 2nd. (revised) ed.

Whatever the original merits of McKenzie's thesis, few commentators now accept that 'the distribution of power within the two major parties is the same.' A theme of this unit will be that despite some similarities in the power structure of the two major parties, caused in part by the British parliamentary system, there are major differences which have in many respects increased in the last decade. While the Conservative Party can be seen as a pyramid, with power and policy-making firmly in the hands of the leader (as long as he or she is electorally successful) the position in the Labour Party is much more complex. The Parliamentary Labour Party and its leaders have never had the same degree of freedom in policy-making as have the Tory leadership. The Labour Party places more value on participation and internal democracy. These features, plus the ever-present ideological divisions, make the job of party management much harder than in the Tory Party.

B. Party structures

A comparison of Labour and Conservative Party structures reveals both similarities and differences. The Labour Party is a federal party, in that there are two ways to join: either as an **individual** member by joining through a constituency party (CLP), or by becoming an **affiliated** member by joining an organisation, such as a trade union or a socialist society (eg the Fabians), which is affiliated to the Labour Party nationally.

The structure of the Conservative Party is somewhat less complex than that of Labour. This is partly the result of the history and ethos of the party and partly because there is only individual membership; members join through their local constituency association. Thus there are no affiliated bodies claiming a share in power.

ACTIVITY 2

Using 6.2 and 6.3 compare the structures of the Labour and Conservative parties:

A   What major similarities and differences can be noted at this stage?

B   What factors might explain your findings in A?

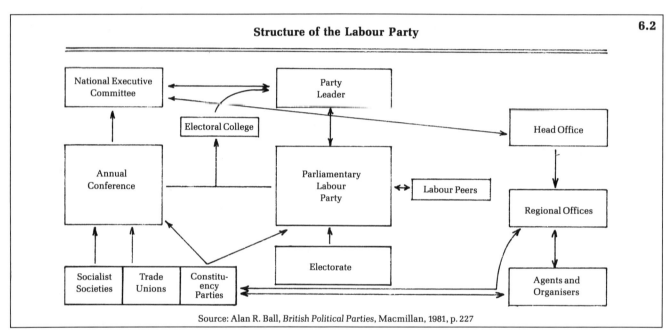

Structure of the Labour Party   6.2

Source: Alan R. Ball, *British Political Parties*, Macmillan, 1981, p. 227

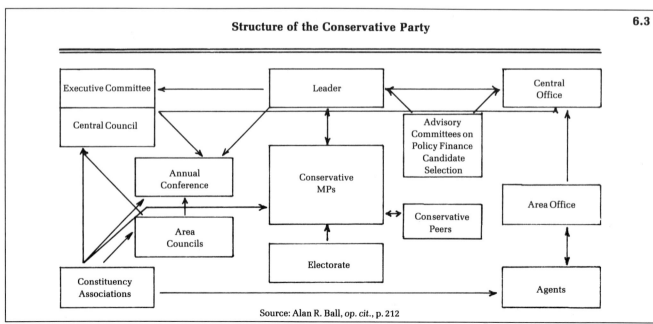

Structure of the Conservative Party   6.3

Source: Alan R. Ball, *op. cit.*, p. 212

C. The party leaders

When the Labour Party has been in power, the leader, as PM, has had a free hand in selecting his ministers. Like Tory leaders, he is limited by political considerations, such as the need to balance left and right, experience and youth, but there are no institutional limitations. In opposition, there are more constraints. The PLP elects the Parliamentary Committee of 15, which forms the nucleus of the Shadow Cabinet to carry out the work of opposing the government in Parliament and whose members act as spokes-persons for Labour in the country. But in reality the leader decides the duties of the Shadow Cabinet and when forming a government is not obliged to retain them in their Shadow posts.

In the Conservative Party, the leader appoints all the senior party officials and thus controls the central administration (in contrast to the position in the Labour party, where administration is under the direction of the NEC, not of the leader). To a much greater extent than in the Labour Party, the Tory leader is seen as the embodiment of the party and as a major (and perhaps dominant) factor in the party's electoral success. Yet despite the tremendous emphasis placed on the leader he or she is not a dictator and must listen carefully to opinion within the party and must keep closely in touch with leading colleagues and with the MPs. In particular, the leader is judged on his or her ability to win general elections. The failure to achieve success was a major factor in the ousting of Edward Heath in 1975.

ACTIVITY 3

A What image of leadership in the Conservative Party is created by 6.4?

B Using the background information and data 6.4–6.5, how important would you say each of the following was in creating this image:
   (i)   the role of the individual;
   (ii) use of the media;
   (iii) party policy;
   (iv) the institutional structure of the party?
   Explain your answer in each case.

6.4

Margaret Thatcher, dominated by a video image of herself, addresses the Brighton conference.

Source: The Independent, 15.10.88

6.5

Thatcherism

She has a set of themes she wishes to see embodied in government policy. They do not amount to an ideology but form a more coherent pattern than the views of most previous Prime Ministers. They constitute a melange of her instincts, lessons from her upbringing, gleanings selected from the writings of a variety of 'new right' writers, ideas from various think-tanks and intellectuals she cultivates in order to stay in touch with current thinking, advice from her Number 10 staff, and above all the policies of her party. This variegated mixture is moulded into Thatcherism by a shrewd politician who watches closely trends of public opinion, and drifts of mood and views within her parliamentary party.

Source: G. W. Jones, 'Cabinet Government and Mrs Thatcher', *Contemporary Record*, Vol 1, 1987

ACTIVITY 4
Study data 6.6–6.9

A How can the institutional structure of the Labour Party be used to explain the predicament of the party leadership as shown by data 6.6?
B Using 6.4–6.9, identify the differences and similarities between styles of leadership in the two major parties.
C How would you explain your answer to B?

6.6

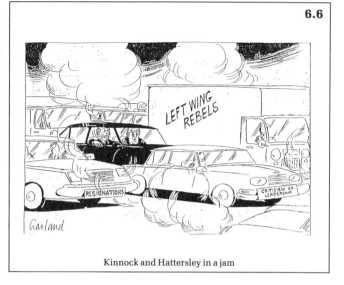

Kinnock and Hattersley in a jam

6.7

6.8

NEIL CRUSHES LEFT

NEIL Kinnock yesterday crushed a Left wing bid to torpedo Labour's new-look defence policy.

He again said that no future Prime Minister needs to answer the question: "Would you press the nuclear button?"

And Labour's national executive voted 20 to 4 against a Left attempt to make him promise publicly that a Labour government would never use the bomb.

Mr Kinnock said he would aim to end the "system of common insecurity" by negotiating a worldwide nuclear ban.

Boost

The Labour Leader got another boost yesterday from a national opinion poll showing that 16 per cent of non-Labour voters were more likely to support the Party after its policy switch.

Only six per cent of Labour voters said they would be less likely to support the party.

Source: *The Daily Mirror,* 10.5.89

6.9

A Labour leader in power

The government cannot be given instructions by the NEC or the Conference. The Prime Minister is more than a party leader; he is responsible to Parliament and the nation. He must always have in mind what is in the national interest, even if that means a clash with the party. The PLP must interpret Conference decisions in the light of circumstances; they are a guide, not a mandate.

Source: adapted from Harold Wilson, *The Governance of Britain,* Weidenfeld and Nicholson, 1976, pp. 162–4

Until 1981 the Labour leader was elected solely by his fellow MPs, but there developed a widespread feeling in the party that the electorate should be widened to give a role to the affiliated organisations and the constituency activists. So in 1981 an **electoral college** was established in which the leader and deputy leader are now elected. The unions have 40% of the vote, with 30% each for the PLP and the CLPs. In 1983 Neil Kinnock was elected leader and Roy Hattersley deputy leader (the 'dream ticket' as it was called).

The Conservative leader has been elected by the parliamentary party since 1965. Before that there was no formal procedure, the leaders were said to have 'emerged' as the result either of being nominated by their predecessor or by a highly secret process of discussions among leading Tories. The last such leader to emerge was Sir Alec Douglas Home in 1963, who until then had been a peer. The controversy was such that a method of election was adopted two years later.

ACTIVITY 5

Study the background information and data 6.10–6.11:

A What are the main differences between the current methods of electing leaders in the Conservative and Labour parties?

B What do these differences tell you about the nature of democracy in each party?

C Why did changes in leadership election methods take place in:
   (i)   the Conservative Party in 1965;
   (ii) the Labour Party in 1981?

6.10

Electing a Labour Party leader

The 1983 election was followed almost immediately by an announcement from Michael Foot that he would retire from the leadership at the following party conference. Denis Healey also gave up his post as deputy leader. Within hours there was talk of a 'dream ticket' combining two of the younger members of the party leadership, one of the 'soft left', like Foot himself, and the other more right-wing: these were Neil Kinnock, aged 41; and Roy Hattersley, aged 50. The two of them, it was thought, would reunite the party; and since Kinnock had never served in the Cabinet, he was free of any blame attaching to the last Labour Government. When the annual conference met at Brighton in early October, balloting took place under the new procedure. Kinnock was well ahead of Hattersley, his nearest rival for the leadership, and secured large majorities in all three categories – trade unions, constituency parties and parliamentary party. Hattersley then secured a similar success for the deputy leadership over Michael Meacher, a left-winger who would not have balanced the team.

Source: Henry Pelling, *A Short History of the Labour Party*, Macmillan, 1985, 8th ed., pp. 186–7

6.11

Electing a Conservative leader

The procedure now involves a ballot of all Conservative MPs; to be elected on the first ballot, a candidate must win an overall majority plus an additional 15 per cent of those eligible to vote. If no candidate achieves this on the first ballot, there is a second ballot in which new candidates may stand and in which only an overall majority is necessary for victory. If there is still no winner on this ballot, a final ballot is held; only the candidates with the three highest votes may stand. Electors rank candidates in order of preference and the winner is determined by adding the number of first preferences to the redistributed second preferences on the papers and the third candidate.

Initially the system was intended only for use when the leadership was actually vacant – in other words when a leader had already indicated his intention of resigning. However after the Conservative Party had lost two elections in 1974 there was increased back-bench dissatisfaction with Edward Heath's leadership and a demand for a revision of the rules to allow for annual elections in which the incumbent could be challenged. This change was made in 1975, and in that year Edward Heath was beaten for the leadership by Margaret Thatcher.

Source: Max Beloff & Gillian Peele, *The Government of the UK*, Weidenfeld & Nicholson, 1985, pp. 218–9

D. The parliamentary party

The Parliamentary Labour Party (PLP) is the parliamentary wing of the party. It consists of all Labour MPs and from it the leader draws most of the ministers when the party is in power. The PLP, together with the Constituency Labour Parties, have been at the centre of the debate over power and influence in the party (see 6.12).

The Conservative equivalent consists of all MPs taking the Conservative whip; there is also a role for Conservative peers. Both in rhetoric and reality, power is placed firmly in the hands of the leader. He or she has dominance in policy-making and is responsible for drawing up the manifesto. Both parties have organisations which convey MPs' feelings to the leadership. Data 6.14 describes the work of the 1922 Committee which organises backbench opinion in the Conservative Party.

ACTIVITY 6

A   What does the writer of 6.12 see as the main problem within the Labour Party?

B   How much power does this suggest the PLP has?

C   Using data 6.14 describe the organisation through which Conservative back-benchers influence the leadership. How much influence over policy does this suggest a Tory backbencher has?

D   Using data 6.12–6.14 would it be true to say that 'Conservative MPs give full allegiance to their leaders while the PLP lacks discipline'?

6.12

Dear Sir,
Today the Labour Party is often more successful in local elections than parliamentary ones in the same constituencies. This must, in part, be due to the fact that the electorate is not faced with the spectacle of Labour councillors habitually speaking and acting in public against the group's decisions. Unfortunately, this is not the case with some members of the PLP.

The constant stream of rebellions and indeed, some resignations, owe more to certain MPs' self-advancement in Parliament than they do to a genuine attempt at resolving the problems of our people in this country.

I must emphasise that the ordinary members and supporters of the Labour Party cannot wait while some members of the PLP indulge in egotistical histrionics instead of standing squarely behind the elected leadership of Neil Kinnock and Roy Hattersley in presenting a co-ordinated and disciplined attack on Thatcherism.

Yours faithfully,
Councillor JIM KEIGHT
Leader
Knowsley Council

Source: *The Independent*, 19.12.88

6.13

Lords encouraged to take up campaign for dog register

THE Government came close to defeat yesterday when MPs voted 159 to 144 to reject a proposal for the introduction of a national dog register. The Government has narrowly resisted pressure from Tory rebels, backed by the RSPCA, for a registration scheme, thought necessary since the abolition of the dog licence, 15 months ago.

The sponsor of the proposal, Dame Janet Fookes, Tory MP for Plymouth Drake, has now urged sympathetic peers to take up the cause when the Local Government and Housing Bill goes to the Lords.

Source: adapted from *The Daily Telegraph*, 16.6.89

6.14

The 1922 Committee

The 1922 Committee is the channel of communication between backbenchers and the leadership, and although it does not use formal votes and resolutions as the Labour Party's committees do, the character of its discussions conveys to the leader the impact which his policies are having in the parliamentary party. The 1922 Committee meets weekly, and when the Conservatives are in opposition the leader and the front-bench spokesmen attend its meetings. If the Conservative Party is in power, however, the members of the administration do not attend and the 1922 Committee becomes the forum solely of backbench opinion. The 1922 Committee's influence is veiled and discreet but nevertheless extensive. It can be assessed from the experience of the leadership crisis of 1974–5, when it was the 1922 Committee which initiated the changes in the rules for election to the leadership to enable an incumbent leader's position to be challenged. And of course the Committee's name commemorates what was probably the most important exercise of backbench power in twentieth-century peace-time history – the decision by Conservative MPs not to support the continuation of the Lloyd George coalition. The 1922 Committee was formed out of the Conservative members returned at the subsequent election.

Source: Beloff & Peele, *op. cit.*, pp. 218–9

E. The extra-parliamentary party

Both the Labour and Conservative Parties have developed mass organisations outside Parliament. The nature of each has been shaped by historical development.

The Conservative or Tory Party has a long history within Parliament stretching back to the seventeenth century. However, it was not until the extension of the franchise in 1867 that an extra-parliamentary organisation was set up to mobilise the new voters. Disraeli founded the National Union with the aim of linking the various constituency associations and uniting Tory support in the country. In 1870 he set up Central Office as the professional head quarters of the party with the principal aim of organising the Tories' electoral effort.

By contrast, the Labour Party began as a pressure group outside Parliament. It was founded in 1900 by a loose alliance of trade unionists, Labour politicians and Socialists. They had varying aims and agreed on little except the need for a party in Parliament to represent the working class. In 1918, the party adopted a constitution, which established a somewhat complex and unwieldy organisational structure, with power distributed throughout the various sections.

In each party there are a number of structures performing different functions. This section looks at the Annual Conference and popular organisation.

The Conference

The **Labour Party Conference** is composed of delegates who are mandated (instructed) by their CLP, Union etc to vote on the resolutions discussed. Conference is dominated by the affiliated unions whose votes count for about five-sixths of the total.

The role of Conference in deciding policy is ambiguous and a matter of controversy (see data 6.17). Resolutions are submitted by CLPs and affiliated organisations and are discussed and voted upon. Any resolution which receives a two-thirds majority is deemed to be part of the party programme. But, in practice whether it then becomes an item of party policy, and in particular whether it is included in the manifesto is decided by a joint committee of the NEC (National Executive Committee) and the Cabinet (or Shadow Cabinet when the party is not in power). At this stage the leader can exercise considerable influence on the contents of the manifesto.

ACTIVITY 7

See data 6.15 and 6.16.

A   What roles are played by the affiliated unions in the Labour Party?

B   Do you think that this is to the benefit of the Labour Party? Is it in the public interest? Explain your answers.

C   Identify the characters in the cartoon (6.15) and explain what the cartoonist is depicting.

D   How did the Conservative Government justify its decision to require unions to hold ballots on the political levy (6.16)?

E   In 1989 the Commons rejected a House of Lords amendment to the Companies Bill giving share-holders the right to block company donations to political parties. What case could a future Labour Government make for requiring companies to ballot their shareholders and/or employees before contributing?

6.15

6.16

Labour and the unions

The trade unions played a crucial part in the founding of the Labour Party, providing both organisation and a social base. They also had an influence on Labour's ideology, moving Labour decisively away from socialism, making it very much a trade union party.

Union influence has frequently been decisive in the party's history. However, the future of the relationship is uncertain. In 1981 a group of moderate union leaders formed the Trade Unions for a Labour Victory (TULV) to revitalize the links with the party leadership. The radical 1983 manifesto and Labour's massive defeat discouraged them. In 1984, polls showed that in only three affiliated unions did a majority of members wish to retain links with the Labour Party and to pay the political levy. The Tory Government then set out to question the right of affiliated unions to donate funds to Labour by requiring them to ballot their members. But by 1985, 84% of 7,300,000 unionists had voted in favour of retaining the levy, even though large numbers of individual unionists had opted out.

The involvement and support of the unions is crucial to Labour and much anxiety remains that powerful unions such as the electricians, power workers and engineers are tending to act independently of the TUC and are showing little enthusiasm for Labour politics.

Source: Stephen Ingle, *The British Party System*, Blackwell, 1987, pp. 136–8

ACTIVITY 8
Study 6.17

A In what ways might it be misleading to emphasise the democratic nature of the Labour Party?
B Do other data in this section confirm Ingle's view that 'Conference is far less representative . . . than it ought to be'? Explain your answer.

6.17

The Labour Conference

There are two practical limitations upon the supposed status of Conference as a parliament of the party. First is the claim that Conference is far less representative of the movement (and thus less of a parliament) than it ought to be, and second is the argument that Gaitskell put before the Conference on the nuclear issue. There was no doubt, he declared, that the majority of MPs were opposed to unilateralism. 'So what do you expect them to do? Change their minds overnight? . . . What sort of people do you think we are?' MPs could hardly fulfil their duties at Westminster if they were tied to pursuing a policy with which they were fundamentally at odds.

Source: S. Ingle, *op. cit.*, p. 26

The **Conservative Annual Conference** is attended by around 5000, composed of MPs and representatives from constituency associations, Young Conservatives and other organisations in the party. They are not mandated delegates and are free to vote as they choose. Most commentators see the Conference as a rally whose main aim is to mobilise the rank and file to work for a Tory Government. The agenda is tightly controlled by the platform, voting is rare and defeats for the leadership rarer still. But although Conference is generally deferential, the leadership will listen to sustained criticism and in recent years, Conference has become more political (as opposed to social) with speakers ready to take issue with the platform.

ACTIVITY 9
Read data 6.18

A According to the author, what are the main functions of the Tory Conference?
B How have the relations between the leader and Conference changed in recent years?
C Why does the writer believe that Tory Conferences are more successful than Labour Conferences?
D What are the dangers of the Tory approach?

6.18

The Tory Conference

The Tory Conference, though a mainly advisory body, is important as an exercise in public relations, both within the party and with the outside world. Whilst there will be little open criticism of the leadership, a good idea will be given of the mood of the party which may well have an influence on policy, as over issues like immigration and law and order. No sensible leadership will ignore this, though attempts will be made to 'manage' it. Since the time of Heath, Conference has become less passive: votes are more frequent and two motions are selected for debate by a ballot of representatives.

The importance of Conference is indicated by the fact that the leader now attends for the whole time; before Heath, he simply addressed it on the last afternoon. Front-benchers are keen to make a good impression; their contribution can be crucial to their standing in the party and a number of ministers have blighted their careers by a lacklustre performance at a crucial time. On the other hand, figures such as Michael Heseltine have greatly advanced their standing by the way they have handled the party faithful.

Especially in the television age, the rather bland and packaged Tory Conference gives a better impression of the party than does its more openly divided Labour counterpart. It is one thing to believe in party democracy; it is quite another to display divisions before potential voters. The purposes of a Tory Conference are more limited than that of Labour; it is an exercise in displaying enthusiasm rather than a serious discussion of issues and policies. Yet 'packaging' can become counter-productive; the Conference can become merely a 'marketing event' with the public tiring of the image being used to hide the message.

Source: S. Ingle, *op. cit.*

ACTIVITY 10
Read data 6.19

A What evidence is there that the public image of a Tory Conference hides the real nature of grass-roots feeling?

B Why did the Charter Movement have so little effect on the 1987 Conference?

C Using all the data, which would you say was the more democratic organisation – the Conservative or Labour Party Conference? Justify you answer.

6.19

Charter Movement

The Tory Party claims to be the defender of democratic rights, but internal party democracy is extremely limited.

Open splits over policies are rare, and the rights of representatives at Conference are restricted to voting for or against motions; amendments are rarely allowed by the (unelected) chairman.

The tiny Charter Movement, a grass-roots organisation of activists intent on getting more internal democracy in the party, distributed leaflets at the last Conference alleging that the agenda had been fixed by the party hierarchy and that ballots had been rigged. But to such an extent do the representatives accept their role in the party that the activities of Charter cause scarcely a ripple of interests. Party officials reject the claim that the Central Office hierarchy, from the Chairman of the Party (appointed by the Leader) should be elected. They claim that this is a recipe for chaos, in that the right person isn't always elected.

Popular Organisation

In each party there are organisations at constituency level which principally promote its aims, recruit members, raise finance, send delegates to Conference and select candidates for local and parliamentary elections. Since 1980, Labour MPs have had to face compulsory reselection in their constituencies before each election, effectively making the PLP more accountable to the mass party. Unlike the Constituency Labour Parties (CLPs), the Conservative Associations do not claim a share in power.

The National Union of the Conservative Party was set up in 1867 to coordinate the work of the local associations. Its main task was to distribute information and from the beginning it was entirely supportive of the party at Westminster; it was never intended as a vehicle for making the party leadership accountable to the membership.

Labour's National Executive Committee (NEC) has the function of coordinating the main components of the party (see data 6.20). In recent years the NEC has exercised its powers of control over CLPs, particularly over the selection of candidates (see data 6.21).

ACTIVITY 11

A What are the advantages and disadvantages of the present structure of the NEC? (6.20)

B What issues are raised by the imposition of a candidate by the NEC on
   (i)   any CLP
   (ii) the Vauxhall CLP? (6.21)

C Re-read data 6.12. In what ways does this give us a different view of the CLPs to that in 6.21?

D How accurately does 6.23 contrast the activities of the local organisations of the two major parties?

E Using data 6.22, 6.23 and the background information, compare the popular organisation of the Conservative Party with that of the Labour Party. Identify the similarities and differences in the distribution of power between central and constituency organisations in each of the parties.

6.20

The NEC

'The present structure of the NEC', says Kavanagh, 'defies any coherent theory of representation'... Nowadays the NEC is said to comprise four divisions. Division one consists of twelve members nominated by the unions from among their delegates and elected by the whole union delegation at the Party Conference. Division two consists of one member, nominated by the socialist and co-operative societies from among their delegates and elected by their delegations. Division three consists of seven members elected by the constituency delegations from among their number (though constituency parties may also nominate their MP or parliamentary candidate). Division four consists of five women members, nominated by any affiliated organization. Constituency parties may nominate their female MP or parliamentary candidate. This division is elected by Conference as a whole. To these members are added the leader and deputy leader of the party sitting ex officio and the prestigious post of party treasurer, elected by the whole Conference.

Source: S. Ingle, *op. cit.*, pp. 128–9

6.21

The Vauxhall by-election

The Labour leadership out-manoeuvred black supporters and left-wingers... over the imposition of Kate Hoey, a loyal Kinnock supporter, as the official party candidate for the Vauxhall by-election in south London.

The leadership's swift action in imposing a candidate in the face of protests by the Vauxhall Labour Party did nothing to reduce the deep resentment among black Labour supporters. Bernie Grant, the MP for Tottenham: 'We think the Labour Party is no longer committed to racial equality and that the party does not want any more black Members of Parliament, because if you cannot get a black MP for Brixton with the highest concentration of black people, then they really don't want any black MPs.'

The row with the leadership arose when the National Executive excluded from the shortlist Martha Osamor, a left-wing black activist, despite her winning the majority of nominations from wards and trade unions, Vauxhall Labour Party voted 33–10 to call on the leadership to supply another black candidate. But the leadership carried out a contingency plan by convening an emergency meeting of its national selection panel and selecting Ms Hoey.

Source: 'Vauxhall selection fuels black supporters' anger', Colin Brown, *The Independent*, 19 May, 1989.

6.22

Conservative constituency associations

Conservative constituency associations are run by Executive Councils which contain representatives from the constituent elements of the party: Young Conservatives, Conservative Clubs and ward and district branches. They play an important role in the selection of parliamentary candidates under the overall supervision of the central party organisation, which maintains a list of approved candidates.

Source: B. Coxall and L. Robins, *Contemporary British Politics*, Macmillan, 1989, p. 241

6.23

F. Conclusion

The work you have done in this unit should enable you to draw some conclusions about the balance of power between the parliamentary and extra-parliamentary wings within each major party, and to draw comparisons between them. In this way, R. T. McKenzie's thesis may be tested.

ACTIVITY 12
Refer back to 6.1. How accurate is the McKenzie thesis, that 'the distribution of power within the two major parties is the same'? Support your answer with reference to what you have learnt from studying this unit.

Further reading

Alan R. Ball, *British Political Parties: The Emergence of a Modern Party System*, Macmillan, 1987, 2nd. ed.

Max Beloff and Gillian Peel, *The Government of the U.K.: Political Authority in a Changing Society*, Weidenfeld and Nicholson, 1985, 2nd. ed.

Robert Blake, *The Conservative Party from Peel to Thatcher*, Fontana, 1985

W. N. Coxall, *Parties and Pressure groups*, Longman, 1986, 2nd. ed.

Stephen Ingle, *The British Party System*, Blackwell, 1987

Dennis Kavanagh, *Thatcherism and British Politics: The End of Consensus*, O.U.P., 1987

Robert McKenzie, *British Political Parties*, Mercury, 1963, 2nd. (rev.) ed.

Henry Pelling, *A Short History of the Labour Party*, Macmillan, 1985, 8th ed.

Patrick Seyd, *The Rise and Fall of the Labour Left*, Macmillan, 1987

UNIT 7 Political Ideologies

'There are basically only two ways in which to run a country – one is the Socialist way and one is the Conservative way . . .' Margaret Thatcher, *Sunday Times*, 8 May 1988. What, if anything, is the Conservative Party trying to conserve? What does the Labour Party mean when it refers to itself as 'socialist'? Do the terms 'left' and 'right' tell us anything about the two parties, or do they obscure more than they reveal?

Introduction

At its simplest, an ideology comprises an analysis of society, and more loosely, the world it inhabits; a set of prescriptions for that society, and a programme of action. In this sense modern Conservatism and Socialism in Britain are both ideologies. However, most commentators agree that Conservatism is less systematic, and in the past Conservatives themselves made a positive virtue of the fact. By contrast, the appeal of Socialism lay in its advocacy of progress and reform and the planned improvement of the human condition.

The Labour Party was almost completely unprepared for the ideological resurgence of Conservatism that occurred after 1974. Socialists had grown accustomed to their apparent monopoly of the use of terms like 'freedom'. Disliking discussion on 'ends', and increasingly pragmatic in policy, Labour was overwhelmed by Mrs Thatcher.

During the 1979 General Election, it was the Labour Party who were defending the political consensus, and the Conservatives who were offering radical reform. Since that time, the Conservatives have referred to the 'Thatcher Revolution', and have borrowed the language of the '60s to talk of 'the long march through the institutions'. Margaret Thatcher herself has spoken of her wish to 'get rid of Socialism'. 'Thatcherism' appeared to be a new phenomenon, but even by the later 1980s, not every Conservative MP was an unreserved enthusiast.

ACTIVITY 1

A What is the similarity between Margaret Thatcher's assertion in data 7.1 and Sir Robin's question about the 'death of Socialism' in the cartoon (7.2)?

B In what ways can these be related to the changing ideological positions of the Labour and Conservative parties in the 1970s and 1980s?

7.1

The Labour Party is like one of these prehistoric mammoths we sometimes discover trapped in Siberian ice.

Source: Margaret Thatcher, *Conservative Party Conference*, 1988

7.2

THAT'S MUCH BETTER.... AAH! HATTERSLEY!! YOU'RE A **FAT SOD!!** WHAT HAVE YOU GOT TO SAY TO **THAT ???**

SPIN

I THINK WHAT WE'RE TALKING ABOUT HERE IS A **FOUR HORSE SCENARIO** IN A **TWO HORSE** HANDICAP WITH A LOT OF **FUNNY MONEY** RIDING ON A **DRUGGED WHIPPET** ...

I SEE

...SO YOU'RE SAYING THAT WE'RE WITNESSING THE **DEATH OF SOCIAL--ISM** HERE ?

I WASN'T AWARE THAT I'D SAID **THAT**, SIR ROBIN....

NORMAN TEBBIT ?? **IAN WRIGGLESWORTH** ??

YOU'RE **ABSOLUTELY RIGHT,** SIR ROBIN!!

BUT BUT BUT BUT BUT...

Source: *The Guardian*

A. British Conservatism

Conservatism as an ideology has a long history, receiving its clearest formulation in Edmund Burke's *Reflections on the Revolution in France*, published in 1798. It encompasses a complex set of ideas about the nature of man, society and political change. It is normally associated with the right wing of the political spectrum. Data 7.4 gives one author's view of the main principles of Conservatism. Kirk regards the six principles as broad descriptions rather than fixed definitions. This section relates these to the **libertarian** and **organic** models of Conservatism, as defined in 7.3.

ACTIVITY 2

A Look at Kirk's Six Principles (7.4) and see which of them are applicable to the libertarian and organic conceptions of Conservatism (7.3), eg

Libertarian	Organic
1	
2	
3	
4	
5	
6	

B What do you conclude from this analysis about Kirk's view of Conservatism?

7.3

Libertarian and organic models of Conservatism

Libertarian Conservatism views society as a collection of self-sufficient individuals, and so relies upon the bourgeois or classical liberal rhetoric of free enterprise, self-help and limited government. There is, however, an alternative model within Conservatism whereby society appears as an interconnected whole bound by a network of reciprocal rights and obligations. The wealthy and powerful, in this organic conception, have an overall responsibility for the common welfare.

Source: Robert Eccleshall, in Eccleshall *et al, Political Ideologies,* Hutchinson, 1984

7.4

Six principles of Conservatism

1. Conservatives generally believe **that there exists a transcendent moral order**, to which we ought to try to conform the ways of society. A divine tactic, however dimly perceived, is at work in human society...

2. **The principle of social continuity**. Order and justice and freedom... are the artificial products of a long and painful social experience... necessary change ought to be gradual...

3. **The principle of prescription**... we are unlikely... to make any brave new discoveries in morals or politics or taste... We do well to abide by precedent, precept, and even prejudice.

4. **The principle of prudence**. Any public measure ought to be judged by its probable long-run consequences, not merely by temporary advantage or popularity. Human society being complex, remedies can-not be simple if they are to be effective...

5. **The principle of variety**. Conservatives feel affection for the variety of long-established social institutions and modes of life, as distinguished from the narrowing uniformity and deadening egalitarianism of radical systems. For the preservation of a healthy diversity in any civilisation, there must survive orders and classes, differences in material condition, and many sorts of inequality.

6. **The principle of imperfectibility**. Man being imperfect, no perfect social order can ever be created... All that we can reasonably expect is a tolerably ordered, just, and free society, in which some evils, maladjustments and suffering continue to lurk. By proper attention to prudent reform, we may preserve and improve this tolerable order.

Source: adapted from Kirk, R. *The Portable Conservative Reader*, Penguin, Hammondsworth, 1982

In recent years, a 'New Right' ideology has emerged within the Conservative Party. It is hostile to *Socialism* but has also been critical of post-war Conservative policies. It is examined in data 7.5.

ACTIVITY 3

A   Which of the principles of Conservatism outlined in data 7.4 would seem to be acceptable to the New Right (see data 7.5) and which would it reject?

B   Are the ideas of the New Right closer to the 'libertarian' model or to the 'organic' model of Conservatism (7.3)?

7.5

The New Right

The main target of the New Right has been social democracy. Not merely the party and trade unions of organised labour but also the willingness of Conservative governments since the war to accept social democratic policies and goals, and to work within social democratic constraints. A constant complaint has been that since 1945 the Conservative leadership has constantly betrayed Conservative principles by acquiescing in the steady consolidation of the power of organised labour and the social democratic state . . . collectivism has steadily increased, economic liberty has been undermined, the economy as a result has declined and political freedom itself placed in jeopardy.

Source: Andrew Gamble, *Britain in Decline*, Macmillan, 1981

B. Thatcherism

Often closely associated with the New Right, Thatcherism, could be considered an ideology in its own right. Essentially it is a blend of neo-conservative, neo-liberal and Tory ideas (see data 7.7). Since 1979, Conservative Governments, under the premiership of Margaret Thatcher, have pursued policies which reflect this brand of British Conservatism. Reactions to Thatcherism are mixed both within and outside the party.

ACTIVITY 4
Study data 7.6–7.7

A   Explain the diagram in data 7.7.

B   Read data 7.6. How would each of the 'three propositions' of Thatcherism apply in practice to council house sales and trade unions? In giving your answers, explain how the words 'markets', 'freedom' and 'choice' would be employed.

C   If Thatcherism represents a change from more traditional Conservative ideology, what do you think Thatcherite Conservatism is trying to conserve?

7.6

Thatcherism

Three connected propositions define the character and appeal of what we know as 'Thatcherism' in economic policy. The first is that the state is bad at running things; the second is that consumer choice is good; the third is that people should be free to enter into economic transactions with each other with as little outside regulation (whether by the state, local authorities or trade unions) as possible . . .

As a general set of political principles, Thatcherism has undoubted appeal. It accords with the instincts of many voters when applied, say, to council house sales or trade union legislation. More than that: Thatcherism enjoys an ascendancy in the very language of politics. Words such as 'markets', 'freedom' and 'choice' have been co-opted to its cause.

Source: Peter Kellner, *The Independent*, 15 February, 1988

7.7

Neo Conservatism

Emphasis on law and order, family, victorian morality etc.

eg Peterhouse Group, Roger Scruton, Victoria Gillick, Peregrine Worsthorne

Toryism

Emphasis on Welfare State and the post-war consensus. Concern for unemployed etc.

eg Heath, Walker, Heseltine, Chris Patten

Neo-Liberalism

Emphasis on European single market, privatisation, free competition etc.

eg Adam Smith Institute, Centre for Policy Studies, Nicholas Ridley, John Redwood

To what extent do political ideologies readily translate into practical policies? One of the central assertions of Thatcherism is that the activities of the state should be 'rolled back', or curtailed, as a precondition of both enterprise and freedom. Study data 7.8 to 7.10.

ACTIVITY 5

A What effect would the abandonment of a policy of full employment have on the provision of unemployment benefit for the long-term and young unemployed? (7.8)

B What has gone 'wrong' with the National Health Service? (7.9)

C In what ways do the NHS recommendations of the right-wing Adam Smith Institute (data 7.10) appear to go against the principles of Thatcherism?

7.8

The post-war consensus

The post-war Welfare State was founded on four main assumptions: that government would pursue a policy of full employment; that there would be a comprehensive health service, free at the point of use; comprehensive insurance against unemployment; and social security provision against poverty.

It was believed that poverty would soon be eradicated. Full employment and a growing economy would mean that most workers would be contributing towards unemployment insurance, and would receive benefits during periods of temporary unemployment. There would be diminishing calls upon social security. Full employment would also mean a decline in poverty-related diseases, and thus in calls upon the National Health Service.

With unemployment over 1 million, the 1974–79 Labour Government abandoned the commitment to full employment. In the 1980s, under the Thatcher Government, official unemployment rose to over 3 million.

7.9

NHS funding

First, the resources of the NHS need to grow by at least 2% a year, in real terms, to keep pace with the extra demands generated by a steadily ageing population, the pace of medical advance and the meeting of priority aims like the development of home kidney treatment and community care.

Second, with wages making up 70% of its bills, NHS costs usually rise significantly faster than the general inflation index, especially since the government almost always concedes NHS pay awards above the inflation rate (though it then refuses to fund them fully.)

Taken together these two reasons explain why, though more money in real terms has been allocated to hospitals during the Thatcher years, there has still been a significant shortfall in hospital funding in every year since 1981.

Source: *Sunday Times*, 24.1.88

7.10

Radical right theorists praise NHS care record

THE National Health Service gives people a sense of security, has an astonishingly good record of primary health care, is run by some talented managers and is not all that expensive.

This enthusiastic tribute to the beleaguered NHS comes today from a most surprising quarter – the free-marketeer Adam Smith Institute.

In a report by the institute, two of the radical right's leading theorists say they want to protect the NHS's achievements and see "a continued health service, funded out of taxation, free at point of supply, and one which will genuinely be the envy of mankind".

The report is the latest in a series outlining the institute's plans for introduction in the NHS of American-style health management units (HMUs) to act on behalf of patients to purchase services from competing hospitals and doctors.

Source: *Guardian*, 11.5.88

ACTIVITY 6

A   What is meant by the phrase '. . . the old culture of sullen dependency' (data 7.11)? What aspects of Conservative social security policy is the cartoonist emphasising?

B   Describe the trend in public (ie state) expenditure since 1973 (data 7.12). To what extent has the state been 'rolled back' since 1979?

C   Is there anything that Mrs Thatcher would consider the state was good at doing?

7.11

One cartoonist's view of the changes in social security entitlement introduced in 1988

Source: Steve Bell, *The Guardian*, 14.4.88

7.12

Public expenditure as a percentage of Gross Domestic Product

1973–74	42.50		1982–83	46.75
1974–75	48.		1983–84	46.
1975–76	48.50		1984–85	46.25
1976–77	46.		1985–86	44.50
1977–78	42.50		1986–87	43.75
1978–79	43.25		1987–88	41.75 (1)
1979–80	43.50		1988–89	41.25 (2)
1980–81	46.		1989–90	40.75 (2)
1981–82	46.50		1990–91	40. (2)

1 Estimated out-turn
2 1988 PSBR plans

Source: adapted from *HM Treasury figures*, 1988

7.13

The Argentine cruiser, General Belgrano, sunk by the Royal Navy in the Falklands War, 1982

What have been the effects of Thatcherite Conservative policies on how income and wealth is divided among the population, and do these effects correspond to modern Conservative ideology? Examine data 7.14 to 7.18.

ACTIVITY 7

A What percentage of privatised shares were owned by social class C2 in 1987? (7.14) Would you expect C2 to be traditionally a share-owning class?

B What percentage of marketable wealth was owned by
(i) the most wealthy 10%
(ii) the most wealthy 50%
in 1971 and 1985? (7.15)

C Using 7.16 and 7.17 analyse the impact of taxation on the incomes of households. How has this changed since 1976?

D Using your answers to A and C, which groups have gained and lost since 1979?

E Study 7.18. Does the redistribution of wealth seem to have affected voting behaviour since 1983? Why should you treat your conclusions with caution?

7.14

Share ownership of privatised companies and Trustee Savings Bank by social class

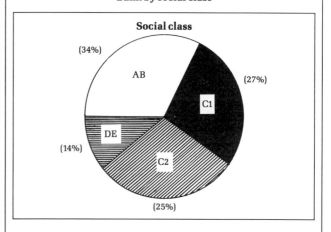

Key

AB – Professional/managerial
C1 – White collar
C2 – Skilled workers
DE – Semi-skilled/unskilled

Source: adapted from *Social Trends*, 18, 1988

7.15

Distribution of wealth

UNITED KINGDOM	PERCENTAGES AND £s BILLION			
	1971	1976	1981	1985
Marketable wealth Percentage of wealth owned by:				
Most wealthy 1%	31	24	21	20
Most wealthy 5%	52	45	40	40
Most wealthy 10%	65	60	54	54
Most wealthy 25%	86	84	77	76
Most wealthy 50%	97	95	94	93
Total marketable wealth (£s billion)	140	263	546	863

Source: *Social Trends*, 19, 1989

7.16

Distribution of original and disposable household income

QUINTILE GROUPS OF HOUSEHOLDS

	Bottom fifth	Next fifth	Middle fifth	Next fifth	Top fifth	
Original income[1]						
1976	0.8	9.4	18.8	26.6	44.4	100.0
1981	0.6	8.1	18.0	26.9	46.4	100.0
1985	0.3	6.0	17.2	27.3	49.2	100.0
1986	0.3	5.7	16.4	26.9	50.7	100.0
Disposable income[2]						
1976	7.0	12.6	18.2	24.1	38.1	100.0
1981	6.7	12.1	17.7	24.1	39.4	100.0
1985	6.5	11.3	17.3	24.3	40.6	100.0
1986	5.9	11.0	16.9	24.1	42.2	100.0

1 Total current income.
2 Total current income less UK taxes on income, employees national insurance contributions, and contributions of employees to occupational pension schemes.

Source: *Social Trends*, 19, 1989

7.17

Shares of total income tax liability

United Kingdom	Percentages and £ billion		
	1986–87	1987–88[1]	1988–89[1,2]
Quantile groups of taxpayers			
Top 1 per cent	14	15	13
Top 5 per cent	29	30	28
Top 10 per cent	40	41	39
Next 40 per cent	43	42	44
Lower 50 per cent	17	17	17
All taxpayers (£ billion = 100%	41.9	44.1	44.5

1 Estimates
2 Since 1979 the basic rate of tax has dropped from 33% to 25% and the higher rates of tax of up to 83% have been replaced by one 40% rate.

Source: *Inland Revenue*, Social Trends, 1989

7.18

Vote by social class (%)

	Con	Lab	Lib/SDP	All
Professional/managerial				
Vote in 1987	59	14	27	
Change from 1983	−3	+2	—	
Office/clerical				
Vote in 1987	52	22	26	
Change from 1983	−3	+1	+2	
Skilled manual				
Vote in 1987	43	34	24	
Change from 1983	+4	−1	−3	
Semi-skilled/unskilled manual				
Vote in 1987	31	50	19	
Change from 1983	+2	+6	−8	
Unemployed				
Vote in 1987	**32**	**51**	**17**	
Change from 1983	**+2**	**+6**	**−9**	

Source: I. Crewe, *Social Studies Review*

How effective has Thatcherism been in re-shaping the context and content of British politics since 1979? Do the changes amount to 'a revolution'? Data 7.19–7.23 give different views of Mrs Thatcher's version of Conservatism.

ACTIVITY 8
Study data 7.19 to 7.23

A In the light of the statistical information (data 7.14–7.18), how do you assess the statement by Michael Fallon MP?
B Which 'successes' do you think John Biffen wishes to conserve? How would they be secure? (7.20)
C In what sense does 'History' begin in 1979? (7.21)
D Explain what you understand by 'trickle down' theory. What are the objections to it? (7.23)
E What sort of Conservative is Jim Prior? (7.22)
F How accurate is it to talk of the 'Thatcher Revolution'?

7.19

Mrs Thatcher is the ultimate socialist. She's shown that a Conservative Government can re-distribute wealth and ownership in a far more radical way than any Labour Government's achieved in this country, and in a far more radical way than they've ever dreamed was possible.

Source: Michael Fallon, Conservative MP

7.20

...the successes of the last 8 or 9 years are now the elements that one wishes to conserve, and I would have thought one is staking out the political ground where they will be secure.

Source: John Biffen, MP *Talking Politics*, BBC Radio 4 9 April, 1988

7.21

What it boils down to is that Thatcherite Conservatism is basically about conserving the results of Thatcherism. History for some began in 1979.

Source: Robin Oakley, (Political Editor, The Times), *Talking Politics*, BBC R4

7.22

I do not regard the swing to 'Thatcherism' as more than a passing phenomenon in the evolution of the Conservative Party. The art of leadership is to change the mood so that the unacceptable becomes possible. To some extent Margaret Thatcher has achieved this...but Margaret herself has had to trim her policies...

Whatever the temporary mood of the party, one is a conservative because of certain instincts and beliefs about society, about life and about change...you do not leave your party merely because you are at variance with the approach and style of those who are temporarily leading it.

Source: adapted from Jim Prior, *A Balance of Power*, Hutchinson, 1986

7.23

A hunch that what's good for the rich is good for the nation and therefore good for the poor is only a hunch, and a wrong one for which no respectable evidence exists. 'Trickle-down' theory sounds fine, but only until you've read J K Galbraith's homely explanation of it; if you feed horses enough oats, some eventually gets right through the horse and then the sparrows have their turn. It's a theory that is said to have more believers among horses than sparrows.

Source: Gordon Brown, Labour MP, *Sunday Times*, 15.5.88

C. Socialism and Social Democracy

Although Socialism has its roots in the political theory of the eighteenth century, it is more closely associated with the period of industrialisation which Britain and Europe experienced during the nineteenth century.

One definition of Socialism is given in data 7.24. The fundamental belief in the state ownership of the means of production and equality is contrasted with the principles of Social Democracy (7.25).

ACTIVITY 9

Compare the description of Socialism (data 7.24) with the description of Social Democracy (7.25). What differences do you notice?

Socialism **7.24**

...a politico-economic system where the state controls, either through planning, or more directly, and may legally own, the basic means of production. In so controlling industrial, and sometimes agricultural plant, the aim is to produce what is needed by the society without regard to what may be most profitable to produce...All versions...expect to produce an egalitarian society, one in which all are cared for by society, with no need either for poverty, or the relief of poverty by private charity...

Source: Robertson, D., *Dictionary of Modern Politics*, Europa Publications, London, 1986

> **7.25**
>
> ### Social Democracy
>
> ...a label used to indicate a reformist and non-Marxist left-of-centre party, one which differs from moderate Conservatism only in relatively marginal ways. A typical social democrat party...will probably espouse some degree of nationalisation, but do so more in terms of the capacity for organised planning of the economy, or the guaranteed production of public utilities, than from any theoretical opposition to private property as such. Again, a social democratic party is likely to opt for higher and more proportional direct taxation, for taxes on industry and commerce, on the grounds of social justice. Such a party will prefer to balance towards redistribution, especially through an organised welfare state, but will not make equality a primary goal in its own right.
>
> Source: Robertson, D., *op. cit.*, 1986

D. Is the Labour Party socialist?

The origins of the Labour Party lie with the formation in 1900 of the **Labour Representation Committee**. In 1918, the Labour Party adopted its present **socialist** constitution. The best-known element is Clause IV (7.28) which is printed on every membership card.

In practice, the membership of the Labour Party constitutes 'a broad church', containing both socialists and social democrats. Until the late 1970s, there were even some liberals – attracted by the Party's programme in the 1930s and 1940s, at a time when the Liberal Party itself seemed in terminal decline.

The Fabian Society is a Labour Party 'think-tank': a vehicle for individuals to express ideas, while it has no collective views of its own. Up to the 1940s, it was dominated by Sidney and Beatrice Webb, and their view of Socialism was of a society run by disinterested professional administrators in the interest of all. Herbert Morrison, deputy leader of the Party after the War, a man not troubled by philosophical doubts, had an uncomplicated vision of Socialism. It took the form of a series of corporate organisations, run by Boards of Directors responsible to Ministers, and with aims laid down by Act of Parliament. The post-war Labour Government created several such corporations to run the newly-nationalised sectors of the economy.

ACTIVITY 10

A   Make a copy of the grid shown in 7.26. On it place:
:   (i)   Clause IV,
:   (ii) the definition of Social Democracy (7.25).

B   The Labour Party has had three major periods of government since 1945: 1945–51; 1964–70 and 1974–79. With the help of data 7.27 place each of the governments on the grid.

C   Is 'Labourism' (see data 7.29) the same as Socialism? Explain your answer.

D   Suggest examples of 'extra-parliamentary forms of working-class political activity' which might be described as socialist (7.29).

E   See data 7.30. Why do you think Herbert Morrison defined Socialism in this way? Explaining your answer, say whether or not you think it is a satisfactory definition.

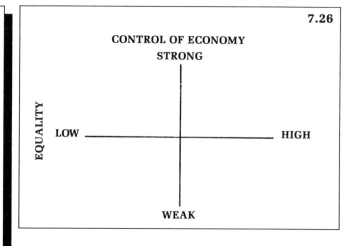

7.26

CONTROL OF ECONOMY
STRONG

EQUALITY

LOW ——————————— HIGH

WEAK

7.27

Labour Government policies

1945–51 Nationalisation of Bank of England, coal, railways, gas, electricity, steel; creation of NHS and National Insurance; Austerity programme in economy.

1964–70 Introduction of comprehensivisation in schools; Race Relations Act; devaluation of the pound; statutory wages policy; Equal Pay Act; renationalisation of steel.

1974–79 Sex Discrimination Act; Employment Protection Act; Social Contract; nationalisation of ship building, aircraft production and Leyland cars; public spending cuts.

7.28

Clause IV

To secure for the workers by hand or by brain the full fruits of their industry and the most equitable distribution thereof that may be possible upon the basis of the common ownership of the means of production, distribution and exchange, and the best obtainable system of popular administration and control of each industry or service.

Source: *Labour Party Membership Card*

7.29

Labourism

...that workers have taken the wage relationship under capitalism as unalterable, and have concentrated their industrial and political efforts on improving their lot within it. In addition the belief has predominated that politics is about PARLIAMENTARY action; and any widespread knowledge of, or interest in, extra-parliamentary forms of working-class political activity has been limited...

Source: David Coates, *Labour in Power?*, Longman, 1980

7.30

'Socialism is what the Labour Party happens to be doing at any one time.'
Source: Herbert Morrison

ACTIVITY 11

A Read data 7.31 and then compare the definition of 'Statism' (7.32) with the definitions of Socialism and Social Democracy (7.24 and 7.25) and with Clause IV (7.28). Why do socialists seem so committed to the idea of central planning?

7.32

Statism

The belief that planning, especially economic and social planning, should be placed as far as possible in the hands of the central government authorities.

Source: Roberts, G. K., *A Dictionary of Political Analysis*, Longman, 1971

7.31

Labour's Programme 1973 adopted the ideas of Tony Benn and Stuart Holland, calling for an extension of nationalisation, – a National Enterprise Board to invest in the profitable parts of the private sector, and *planning agreements* with the largest companies so that their profits, production and investment were in line with government economic planning.

E. Market Socialism

In the late 1980s, debate over the future direction of Labour, ie what it actually means by Clause IV, and how it proposes to achieve it, seemed to be polarised between the left and the right of the party; between the views of Tony Benn, and those of Roy Hattersley and Bryan Gould.

Benn's view of public ownership is a development of his earlier ideas ie the Benn-Holland strategy: greater public ownership; more accountability either to Parliament, party activists or workers; planning agreements. Others close to Benn argue that Labour's appeal ought to be a 'rainbow coalition' of minorities, who together can become an electoral majority. Hattersley regards himself as the inheritor of Crosland's mantle, reaffirming the principles of Clause IV, but reinterpreted for the realities of the 1990s. Hattersley and Gould have both attempted to equate freedom with equality, seeking to wrest back the concept of freedom from the New Right. Gould has argued for a proportion of shares in private companies to be held by its workers. No individual worker would be able to trade them on the Stock Exchange, but they would be held collectively, and used to allow the workforce, as share holders, to influence the direction of company policy. In Sweden, the Social Democrat Government levies a tax on companies to allow the trade unions to buy blocks of shares for similar purposes.

The reinterpretation of Clause IV to suit the realities of the 1990s was confirmed by Labour's 1987–1989 Policy Review, but was largely obscured by the far greater, and symbolic, reinterpretation of defence policy. The change is summed up by an abandonment of the assumption that eventually most of industry would be publicly owned. Labour is seemingly committed to the maintenance and promotion of private sector enterprise, and the role of market forces in economic development. The realities of 1992 and the Single European Act are markedly different from those of 1945: heavy industry is no longer the key factor in economic development, and a search for the 'commanding heights' of the economy might end up looking at the City of London, *Macdonalds* and the *Bodyshop*. 51% of share ownership is unnecessary if you have one 'Golden Share' (as the Tories did with many privatised companies.) The centrally planned economies of Eastern Europe no longer provide a credible alternative: they are inefficient, debt-ridden and are being dismantled. The term 'Market Socialism' has been coined to describe the changes in Labour's ideas (and in those of socialist parties abroad.) Data 7.33 to 7.35 explore and comment upon this concept.

ACTIVITY 12

Study the background information and data 7.33–7.35

A   How consistent are the views of Benn, Hattersley and Gould with the definition of Socialism in data 7.24?

B   What explanation (if any) is Steve Bell offering for the Labour Party's adoption of Market Socialism? (7.35)

C   Write a script for a short Labour Party political broadcast which attempts to show that the ideas of 'Market Socialism' are different from, and preferable to, 'Thatcherism'.

D   Write a brief newspaper article arguing that 'Market Socialism' and 'Thatcherism' are similar.

7.33

The better choice for one and all

The truth is that we have found it particularly difficult to respond to the changes in people's expectations which have occurred during the 1980s. Should we reject them . . . or should we accommodate them . . . and adapt them . . . ?

Nowhere is this more true than on the issue of individual choice . . . an issue which the Tories have made very much their own. Tory propaganda has constantly emphasized their zeal in extending, through measures like council house sales and privatisation, the choices apparently available for ordinary people . . . The Tories have arguably extended the mechanisms of choice but have failed to ensure that these increased opportunities are not limited to and exploited by a privileged minority . . . choice does not exist unless it can be exercised . . . For many . . . it increases their comparative powerlessness in the face of the increased real choice available to the already powerful.

. . . The people will want something better for the 1990s.

Source: adapted from Bryan Gould, *The Guardian*, 6.2.89

7.34

Market Socialism

The essence of market socialism is that it seeks to reconcile economic freedom with social justice. Both are large terms that require proper definition: economic freedom includes the ability of all, not just the rich, to exercise choice; social justice includes the right of everyone to live in a clean safe environment.

The fundamental difference between market socialism and Thatcherism is this. Thatcherism holds that, in the main, when two people, or groups of people, enter into an economic transaction, only they are affected by it. They should be left alone. The rest of society, represented by the government, has no business interfering.

Market socialism holds that this might be true in the unreal world of pure markets described in undergraduate textbooks, but the real modern world is far more complex. Monopolies are formed. Multinationals stalk the world. Financial power is concentrated in relatively few hands.

Exploitation is rife . . . economic transactions routinely affect people who are not party to them. Pollution provides the obvious example . . . excessive lead in petrol . . . acid rain . . . untreated sewage at the seaside.

Thatcherism argues that, at root, freedom is advanced most surely by the absence of government intercession in our lives. In contrast, market socialism argues that freedom needs to be positively promoted. It seeks to disperse power, attack inequality, widen consumer choice, protect the public interest and encourage competition.

Once the project of socialism is presented in that light, and not as a belief in the universal merits of socialisation of production, the prospects for serious political debate in the 1990s will be transformed.

Source: Peter Kellner, *The Independent*, 15 February 1988

7.35

Source: Steve Bell, *IF . . . Bounces Back*, Methuen, 1987

F. Conclusion

ACTIVITY 13

A The phrase in data 7.36 was one of the aims of 'Labour's Programme 1973', and was also used by Tony Benn. In her speech to the 1987 Conservative Party Conference, Margaret Thatcher used it, claiming it as an effect of her policies. Does this mean that Labour and Conservative share a common purpose? Explain your answer.

B Explain the statement in 7.37 and say whether or not you agree with it.

C In your opinion has Margaret Thatcher been successful in her wish to eradicate Socialism?

7.36

. . . a fundamental and irreversible shift in the balance of wealth and power in favour of working people and their families . . .

Source: *Labour's Programme*, 1973

7.37

Thatcherism has shifted the goalposts and the Labour Party has moved to the right to maintain a chance of scoring.

Further reading

Crosland, A., *The Future of Socialism*, London, 1957
Hall, S. and Jacques, M., *Politics of Thatcherism*, London, 1983
Hayek, F., *The Road to Serfdom*, London, 1949
Kavanagh, D., *Thatcherism and British Politics*, Oxford, 1987
Kirk, R., *Portable Conservative Reader*, Harmondsworth, 1982

UNIT 8 Pressure groups

This unit seeks to test the validity of the argument that pressure groups are too powerful and are harmful to democracy.

Introduction

Pressure groups can be defined as organisations which try to influence government policy on a single issue or a range of related issues. But should governments take any notice of groups which may represent minority viewpoints? For example, should broadcasting policy be influenced by the suggestions of Mary Whitehouse's National Viewers' and Listeners' Association whose membership is mainly middle class and elderly? And, why is it that some groups have more success than others in altering policy? Does this mean that those with little impact on government, like CND, are failures? Central to all these questions is the issue of power. We shall be considering whether pressure groups have too much power over our elected representatives – or whether, in the post-1979 era of 'conviction politics', such groups are actually not powerful enough.

A. Defining pressure groups

The first question to examine is which groups really **are** pressure groups.

ACTIVITY 1

Start by listing groups of any kind which you belong to or are familiar with. Then use the general definition in the introduction to decide which of the groups on your list are pressure groups. Compare the pressure groups with the other groups and suggest any additional differences between them.

What criticisms or changes could be made to the introductory definition of pressure groups?

ACTIVITY 2

A Using data 8.1 as your starting point suggest the main differences between pressure groups and political parties.
B What overlaps might there be between pressure groups and political parties in practice (see 8.2)?

8.1

Pressure groups and political parties

Parties differ from pressure groups in three respects. First, they run candidates at general elections and try to capture political office directly. Some groups sponsor candidates for a political party at elections, but in Britain only the trade unions do this on a large scale. Second, parties have to develop comprehensive programmes of policies to appeal to a majority of the electorate. Groups, by contrast, want to articulate a sectional interest. Finally, a party in government has to accept responsibility for a wide range of policies. Groups are more concerned to influence the policy makers than to seek this responsibility.

Source: adapted from D. Kavanagh, *British Politics, Continuities and Change*, O.U.P. 1985 p.150

8.2

By-election results, 1988

KENSINGTON		%

Sir Brandon Rhys Williams, Bt died on May 18, 1988 and a By-election was held on July, 14 1988

D. Fishburn (Con)	9,829	41.59
A Holmes (Lab)	9,014	38.14
W. Goodhart (SLD)	2,546	10.77
J. Martin (SDP)	1,190	5.04
P. Hobson (Green)	572	2.42
C. Payne (Payne & Pleasure)	193	0.82
'Lord' Sutch (Monster Raving Loony)	61	0.26
J. Duignan (London Class War)	60	0.25
B. Goodier (Anti-Left)	31	0.13
B. McDermott (Free Trade Lib)	31	0.13
R. Edey (Fair Wealth)	30	0.13
W. Scola (Leveller)	27	0.11
J. Crowley (Anti-Yuppie)	24	0.10
J. Connell (Stop ITN)	20	0.09

Dr K. Trivedi (Independent Janata)	5	0.02
Con majority 815	3.4%	
Electorate 46,419		
Total vote 23,633	Poll 50.9%	

GLASGOW GOVAN		%

The Rt Hon. Bruce Millan resigned on Oct. 19, 1988 to become a European Commisioner and a By-election was held on Nov. 10, 1988.

J. Sillars (SNP)	14,677	48.75
R. Gillespie (Lab)	11,123	36.95
G. Hamilton (Con)	2,207	7.33
B. Ponsonby (SLD)	1,246	4.14
G. Campbell (Green)	345	1.15
D. Chalmers (Comm)	281	0.93
'Lord' Sutch (Monster Raving Loony)	174	0.58
F. Clark (Rainbow)	51	0.17
SNP majority 3,554	11.8%	
Electorate 50,035		
Total vote 30,104	Poll 60.2%	

Source: *Dod's Parliamentary Companion*, 1989

ACTIVITY 3

A Using the categories of pressure groups suggested in data 8.3, suggest your own examples for each category.

B How would the groups illustrated in 8.4 and 8.5 be classified according to the method described in 8.3?

C Suggest any other ways in which pressure groups could be classified into different categories.

8.3

Classifying groups

Cause groups These are single-issue, politically specific organisations which are concerned with the promotion of policies derived from a shared set of values, beliefs or ideology, eg the Howard League for Penal Reform, the Child Poverty Action Group. These groups often develop with, or have their roots in, charitable organisations.

Interest groups Protectional groups. These are based on multi-functional organisations such as trade unions and professional associations which have a common economic interest.

Non-economic and non-political voluntary associations Based on social groups and groupings such as ramblers, boy scouts, anglers and Anglicans, these engage less regularly in political lobbying as their primary function is neither to protect nor promote.

Source: Malcolm Davies, *The Politics of Pressure*, BBC, 1985

8.4

16 years of misery on condemned estate

1968: Newby Square is built to replace the clearance area known as Little India off Manchester Road.

1982: June 30 – Tenants begin rent strike over demands for compensation for damage to carpets and decorations after flooding hits 18 ground floor maisonettes. They complain that officials failed, despite repeated requests, to carry out an inspection.

August 7 – Housing Services Special Sub-Committee agrees that council should help pay for redecoration and replacement of carpets. Tenants are urged to take out insurance on the property.

August 21 – Tenants occupy Newby Square council office, angry over slow replacement of carpets. Council said it was under no legal obligation to compensate flood victims but would do so 'as a goodwill gesture'.

August 24 – Sit-in continues. Protesters accuse Housing Chairman Coun. Ken Hirts

of 'lying', and challenge him to meet them.

August 25 – Coun. Hirst says protesters 'can sit there all winter if they want...We will not be blackmailed'.

September 14 – National Anti-Dampness Campaign – Shelter-backed – says flats should be repaired or bulldozed. Coun. Hirst says inspection of flats within previous three years had produced 'clean bill of health'. Protesters open their own complaints office.

September 20 – Housing Committee meeting disrupted by hecklers asking why Newby Square question was to be discussed in private. Coun. Hirst asked to resign, and Labour councillors criticised for not supporting tenants earlier.

September 21 – Coun. Abdul Hameed visits the square and reports his 'alarm' at claims that asbestos had been used in construction.

September 25 – Sit-in ends after council agreed to make goodwill payments of £4000.

1983: June 20 – World in Action features 70,000 properties built throughout Britain by Bison Concrete. Interview with former Bison executive who admitted destroying documents dealing with construction faults.

July 13 – Six councillors call for release of month-old report on Newby Square.

July 21 – Report shows that defects would take 'millions' to remedy.

August 2 – Council decides to demolish flats.

October 27 – Tenants assured rehousing office would be set up on the estate.

1984: April 17 – Tenants stage sit-in at housing department and refuse to leave before seeing Director of Housing.

May 30 – Rehousing office opens on the estate. By now 350 families have already moved.

Source: *Politics and You*, BBC Publications, London, 1985, p.8

8.5

Live Aid

B. Why are some groups more successful in influencing government policy?

ACTIVITY 4
List all the strategies a pressure group could use to try to influence government policy. Number the strategies according to which you think are most likely to bring success.

Case-study: National Viewers and Listeners Association.

The NVALA was founded in 1965 with Mary Whitehouse as its President. From an attendance of 2000 at its first meeting the association has grown to a membership of 170,000, on its own estimate. According to an NVALA spokesman, it does not receive much outside funding, so it has to rely mainly on individual donations and £1 membership fees. Successes include:

- 1978   Protection of Children Act – stricter controls over child pornography;
- 1981   Indecent Displays Act – controls over sex shops advertising;
- 1984   Video Recordings Act, introduced by Graham Bright MP – controls established over 'video nasties';
- 1988   Broadcasting Standards Council – set up to monitor sex and violence on television;
           Obscene Publications Act to be extended to broadcasting.

ACTIVITY 5

A   From the background information, and your group's knowledge and views about the issue, how successful do you think the NVALA has been in achieving aims 2 and 3 (listed in data 8.6)?

B   Examine data 8.7 to 8.10. List in order of importance, the reasons why the NVALA was successful in achieving the passage of the Video Recordings Act.

C   From data 8.11 to 8.15 suggest what other reasons there may be for the NVALA's successes in the 1980s.

D   From data 8.16 and 8.17, decide how representative the NVALA is of public opinion.

E   Make out a case suggesting that the NVALA has **either** a useful **or** a damaging effect on democratic decision-making.

8.6

National VALA aims

1 To encourage viewers and listeners to react effectively to programme content.

2 To stimulate public and parliamentary discussion on the effects of broadcasting on the individual, the family and society.

3 To secure effective legislation to control obscenity and pornography in the media – including broadcasting.

Source: NVALA leaflet

8.7

On the election trail

Mary Whitehouse with Steve and Kay Stevens on a tour of twenty marginal constituencies during the 1983 General Election campaign.

8.8

'One of the marginals we went to was Luton which was Mr Graham Bright's seat. I think he'd only got in the previous election by several hundred votes. Now we met him and the local paper came along. We asked him about the video nasties and he was very supportive to what we were doing. All this was in the local paper. He got in again with a majority, I think, of 6000 or something like that. Then when the draw for the private Members' ballot was made at the very beginning of the new session of Parliament, who should be the first one to draw his name out but Graham Bright. So he used his opportunity to introduce a private Member's bill to control video nasties'.

Source: Mrs Whitehouse, quoted in Davies, *Politics of Pressure*, BBC, 1985

8.9

Conservative Party Conference

MARY WHITEHOUSE and National VALA's Chairman Tony Hughes, showed extracts from 'video nasties' at 'fringe meetings' at the recent Conservative party Conference. Mary Whitehouse was surprised at the high attendance at the screenings: '...those who came were absolutely shaken to the core, and then, given that, we wrote to the Party leaders.'

Source: *The Viewer and Listener* (NVALA newsletter), Autumn 1983 and Davies, *op. cit.*

8.10

We will also respond to the increasing public concern over obscenity and offences against public decency, which often have links with serious crime. We propose to introduce specific legislation to deal with the most serious of these problems, such as the dangerous spread of violent and obscene video cassettes.

Source: *Conservative Manifesto*, 1983

8.11

Time and again during the course of the 2nd Reading (3rd April) of Mr Gerald Howarth's bill to tighten up the Obscenity Law and bring broadcasting under its provisions, reference was made to the great number of letters of support for the bill which MPs had received from constituents. AND IT WAS CLEAR FROM WHAT MEMBERS SAID THAT IT WAS THESE LETTERS FROM THE PUBLIC WHICH ENSURED SUCH A HIGH TURN OUT IN THE COMMONS ON A FRIDAY. SO THERE IS A VERY IMPORTANT LESSON TO BE LEARNT FROM THAT AND WE ARE VERY GRATEFUL TO ALL THOSE WHO TOOK THE TROUBLE TO WRITE TO THEIR MPS.

Many hearts must have rejoiced at the announcement that the Tories had committed themselves to action on 'Sex and Violence on TV' in their Election Manifesto. The Tories now have a majority in Parliament and are in a position to make real their promises!

We have known for a long time that Mrs Thatcher has considerable sympathy for our cause but it is very significant that she now feels that public support for it is such that she could safely take an initiative of this kind.

Source: *The Viewer and Listener*, Autumn 1987

Note: Gerald Howarth's bill was defeated, but in November 1988, the Government announced that it would bring in this measure itself.

8.12

Hints on how to organise a successful campaign

1. Write to your local paper using extracts from the information provided here and inviting readers to write to you for information and petition forms etc.
2. Form working party. Organise door to door collection of signatures.
3. Contact local branch of women's and men's organisations, youth clubs etc.
4. Approach local Church leaders and request not only that petitions be made available in Churches but also that Church members collect signatures.
5. Local shops, libraries, Doctors' surgeries, etc., make excellent collecting units.
6. A copy of the address *PORNOGRAPHY, HARM AND WILLIAMS* given by Dr. John Court to a meeting of M.P.s and Peers (July 1st) is available from headquarters (priced 25p). It is essential that every M.P. receives one. **PLEASE SEND FOR A COPY TO SEND TO YOUR M.P.**

Source: *The Viewer and Listener*, Autumn 1980

8.13

Guests at No. 10

In 1988 Ernest and Mary Whitehouse were at 10 Downing Street as guests of Mr and Mrs Thatcher.

8.14

For the last 23 years National VALA has been calling for an Independent Broadcasting Council. Now, at last, the signs are that real public participation will soon become a reality.

Source: *The Viewer and Listener*, Spring 1988

8.15

'We found the permanent staff at the Home Office over the years were almost totally unwilling to listen or to take into account what we were saying. I have to say, in all fairness, that over the last two to three years, particularly since Mrs Thatcher has shown herself to be so concerned and to be so determined to get some action in this field, the Civil Service have decided they'd better sit up and listen a little bit and be a bit more flexible.'

Source: Mrs Whitehouse, quoted in Davies, *op. cit.*

8.16

The NVALA, although a highly articulate group, cannot claim to be representative of the community. Research suggests that its support is mainly middle-class, female and elderly, that it is over-represented by those in rural areas, the clergy, the older-established professions, small businessmen, traders and shopkeepers (*Sunday Times*, 12 Feb. 1978). But its ability to mobilize an important section of public opinion is a formidable weapon. It does not waste time trying to convert those whom it knows are likely to be hostile to its views. It concentrates on the Conservative Party, the churches, the religious press and provincial newspapers, which are likely to be less liberal in outlook than Fleet Street and which welcome contributions from controversial national personalities to relieve the monotony of local tittle-tattle.

Source: G. Alderman, *Pressure Groups and Government in Great Britain*, Longman, 1984, p.111

8.17

Survey findings

	1983	1984	1985	1986	1987
% saying always/mostly wrong					
Pre-marital relations:					
US	36%		36%	36%	
Britain	28%	27%	23%		25%
Extra-marital relations:					
US		87%	87%		89%
Britain	83%	85%	82%		88%
Homosexual relations:					
US		75%	77%		78%
Britain	62%	67%	69%		74%

% saying that pornographic material should be banned altogether	1983	1987	% change 1983–1987
Men:			
Total	25%	33%	+ 8
18–34	6%	11%	+ 5
35–54	18%	30%	+ 12
55 +	52%	61%	+ 9
Women:			
Total	40%	43%	+ 3
18–34	11%	23%	+ 12
35–54	35%	39%	+ 4
55 +	70%	70%	—

Source: *5th British Social Attitudes Survey*, 1988

C. Success or failure? The experience of other groups

ACTIVITY 6

A   How far does the data in 8.18 suggest that the NVALA uses methods which are typical of successful pressure groups?

B   Return to the list you made in Activity 4. What changes would you now make to the order of factors which are important in a pressure group's success?

ACTIVITY 7

A Until 1978 the NVALA had little apparent impact on government policy, yet does this mean it was a failure? Explain your answer.

B Consider the following pressure groups, none of which really changed government policy in the 1980s, and suggest reasons why each group could still argue that it has had some success:
(i) Liveaid;
(ii) Greenpeace;
(iii) the Campaign for Nuclear Disarmament.

8.18

Success in Parliament

'The more astute among the lobbies realise it is not so much the MP who carries weight, it is the minister, and more particularly the civil servant.'
Julian Critchley MP

'At the moment Mrs Thatcher is running the show. If she happens to agree with you that's marvellous. If she doesn't you're in real trouble'.
Des Wilson

'Sometimes a Member of Parliament will come to a pressure group like the Freedom of Information campaign and say: "I wish to get the water authorities re-opened because now they're all operating in secret. Is your campaign interested? Could you present me with a draft bill?"'
Des Wilson

Source: Davies, *op. cit.*

ACTIVITY 8

Test out your ideas on what makes a pressure group successful by reading through data 8.19 to 8.22 and considering these questions:

A In what ways has CND been a failure?
B In what ways has CND been a success?
C How might a pressure group benefit from aiming its campaign primarily at public opinion rather than at the government?

8.19

Success for CND?

From 1980 to 1983 CND was able to demonstrate a massive growth to a national membership of over 250,000, including groups within all the opposition parties and support from about 150 local authorities. As far as public opinion is concerned, CND has enjoyed one major success in helping to mobilise a consistent majority against the American Cruise bases in Britain. In response to CND's opposition to its nuclear defence policies the government has been obliged to adopt a much more open stance and to present to the public intelligent rationales of policy in a way that is quite unprecedented in Britain. CND claims that it was its insistence on nuclear disarmament that forced NATO into the 1987 treaty between the two superpowers. But against that the negotiations were conducted by the Americans alone and this had little to do with pressure from the peace movement.

Source: adapted from Peter Byrd, *Contemporary Record*, Spring 1988

8.20

If the talks between the United States and Soviet governments should fail we shall, after consultation, inform the Americans that we wish them to remove their cruise missiles and other nuclear weapons from Britain... We will cancel Trident and use the money saved to fulfil our role in NATO.

Source: *Labour manifesto*, 1987

8.21

WHY BRITAIN VOTED

(Figures in percentages)

	All	Con	Lab	Lib/SDP
Q: Did Labour's defence policy make you more or less likely to have voted Labour?				
· More likely	18	4	40	12
· Less likely	52	74	17	60
· No difference	29	20	41	26

Source: ITN/Harris exit poll 1987

8.22

D. Are pressure groups too powerful?

ACTIVITY 9
From your work so far, consider whether pressure groups are too powerful.

In the 1970s it was often suggested that interest groups were too powerful. At that time both Labour and Conservative Governments followed a policy of **corporatism**. This meant involving the Confederation of British Industry and the Trades Union Congress in the formation and execution of economic policy. The question 'who governs Britain?' was most frequently posed in relation to the unions. In February 1974, the Conservative Government lost an election called on the issue of the miners' strike: likewise the public sector strikes in the 'winter of discontent' were blamed for the fall of the Labour Government in 1979.

ACTIVITY 10
Read data 8.23–8.25 which present contrasting views of the TUC's power in the 1970s.

A   What are the arguments for and against the idea that 'trade unions governed Britain in the 1970s'? Do you agree with this statement or not?

B   What sort of influence do you think i) unions ii) industrialists and the City should have on economic policies today? (eg public/private ownership; taxes; interest rates; the legal position of trade unions.)

8.23

The Social Contract 1

Labour's legal programme:
(1) *Restored trade union immunities to the 1906 position.*
(2) *Extended the legal rights of individuals*, for example, strengthening their position in relation to unfair dismissal; introducing a system of maternity leave and maternity pay; and developing new rights in the areas of sex and race discrimination and health and safety.
(3) *Introduced a series of collective rights for trade unions and trade unionists*: a new recognition procedure was established; unions were given the right to advance notice and consultation when redundancies were declared.
...A point that should not be overlooked, however, is that many of the changes were required not simply by Congress House but by the need to meet EEC standards.
One reaction was to criticise the new 'corporatism' on the grounds that the unions were endangering their role of representing their members by becoming appendages of the state. Many of the rights were extremely limited, and difficult to enforce with inadequate remedies.
The restrictions the unions accepted set the price of the legislation very high. The new structures could be built on in an anti-union way by a future hostile government. Another response was to argue that trade unions were running the country in defiance of democratic processes. In reality the TUC accepted some of the sharpest real wage cuts this century, rises in unemployment and cutbacks in welfare provision, in return for what amounted to influence not power. Its policies on workers' participation, import controls and planning agreements were not implemented despite tight controls over industrial action and support for restrictive codes on the closed shop, picketing and industrial action. Rank and file resistance to TUC policies erupted in the 1979 'winter of discontent'.

Source: John McIlroy in *Political Issues in Britain Today* (ed. Bill Jones), Manchester University Press, 1985, pp. 76–77

8.24

The Social Contract 2

The proposals of the TUC-Labour Party Liaison Committee formed the basis of both Labour's manifestos in 1974 and of its policies during its first two years of office. This arrangement between the party and the unions was usually referred to as the 'Social Contract'. In return for promises of wage restraint, the party promised to repeal much Conservative legislation and to implement a costly and wide-ranging programme of social policies. Thus the Labour Government repealed the Conservatives' Industrial Relations and Housing Finance Acts, introduced an immediate pensions increase and a reform of the system of state pensions as well as increased subsidies to council tenants and security of tenure to tenants in private furnished accommodation; it also nationalised the aircraft and shipbuilding industries and development land, increased tax rates on higher incomes and (by the Employment Protection Act) gave new rights to workers and trade unions. All these measures, and many more, were directly inspired by the TUC. Yet large wage settlements continued and inflation remained at a higher rate than in most of the industrialised world.

Source: W.N. Coxall, *Parties and Pressure Groups*, Longman, 1986, p. 157

8.25

Insider pressure groups

Corporatism has had much less influence during the years of 'conviction' government under Mrs Thatcher. Elements of it still survive, though, most notably in the close involvement of the National Farmers' Union in the formation of policy at the Ministry of Agriculture.

ACTIVITY 11
Study data 8.26–8.28

A In what ways might a pressure group concerned with the environment or public health attack the insider status of the NFU?

B Defend the NFU's role in government from the point of view of **either** an NFU spokesperson **or** the Agriculture Minister.

8.26

Lobby groups

Incorporating lobby groups into the process of formulating public policy and also in implementing it (the Law Society, for example, runs the Legal Aid scheme), has two advantages for government. Firstly, it results in the provision of a wider set of data because the differing and sometimes competing interests furnish a wealth of technical detail not easily available to government departments. Secondly, it helps to legitimate public policy: by taking part in the formulation of policy, groups, their leaders and members are less likely to criticise and reject governmental decisions.

8.27

'You've got a Ministry that has been working with the NFU for so long that they talk the same language; they go to the same clubs and eat in the same restaurants. They know each other on first-name terms. At this moment, although Friends of the Earth has done all the research on pesticides ... the Government is talking to farmers and the chemical industry in formulating legislative plans. They're not talking to us, we are not on the inside there, we are not part of the club.'

Source: Des Wilson, quoted in Davies *op. cit.*, p. 42

8.28

CURRIE, EGG AND CHICKS

How the farmers made a meal of Edwina

A group of Tory backbenchers, egged on by the poultry lobby, engineered the resignation of the junior health minister. Edwina Currie refused to retract her statement that most of Britain's egg production was infected with salmonella. As egg sales plummeted and unsold stocks rose to 350m last week, the highly organised trade lobby of the poultry farmers used every ounce of their political clout to bring about Currie's downfall.

Source: *Sunday Times*, 18.12.88

Sponsoring MPs

Many MPs receive payments, or contributions to election expenses, from companies or trade unions, and occasionally other pressure groups. In return MPs are expected to further the group's cause.

ACTIVITY 12

A Suggest ways in which MPs could help pressure groups to achieve publicity or affect government policy.

B Examine data 8.29–8.32. What criticism could be made of the payment of MPs by pressure groups? What reforms would you suggest to meet these criticisms?

C How might an MP defend sponsorship by a pressure group?

8.29

MPs interests

SUMBERG, David (Bury South)
Parliamentary Consultant, Northern Independent Bookmakers Association
Parliamentary Adviser to Jackson and Lowe Ltd.
Parliamentary Consultant to Tyndall Holdings, PLC.

STRAW, Jack (Blackburn)
Parliamentary Adviser to the Association of University Teachers.
Sponsored (Parliamentary List) by the General Municipal and Boilermakers Union. No personal payment or personal material benefit is derived.

Source: *Register of Members Interests*, 1988

8.30

There are three or four MPs directly on the pay-roll of tobacco companies, such as Sir Anthony Kershaw, who is paid by British American Tobacco. Other MPs are less obviously linked to the industry through public relations firms hired by the tobacco companies. On 12 June 1981, Sir Anthony Kershaw tabled 27 out of 164 trivial amendments to the Zoo Licensing Bill. The sudden interest in zoos had to do with the subsequent item that day, which was a bill proposed by Laurie Pavitt to eliminate tobacco sponsorship for sport and the arts. Pavitt's bill was not debated owing to lack of time.

Source: Malcom Davies, *op. cit.* pp. 60–61

8.31

Salaries, June 1989

Member of Parliament	– £24,107 pa
Sales manager in computer firm	– £60,000 pa
Average earnings	– £12,500 pa

8.32

'The Police Federation employs Mr Eldon Griffiths. When Mr Griffiths gets up yet again the rest of us MPs are inclined to groan slightly because we know he is doing something for which he is being paid, but having said that, he does, I think, a good job for the police.'

Source: Julian Critchley MP quoted in Davies *op. cit.* p. 60

Professional lobby firms

A new issue since 1979 has been the growth of **professional lobby firms**. These private companies will, for a substantial fee, pursue a campaign on behalf of a pressure group. Is Britain following the example of the United States where policy is often decided by conciliating the various powerful and wealthy lobbies which gain access to Congress? Can any defence be made of allowing wealthy groups to buy themselves expert help in influencing government?

ACTIVITY 13

A What evidence is there in data 8.33–8.36 that professional lobby firms can influence government policy?

B Having examined all the data decide what controls (if any) should exist over professional lobby firms.

8.33

A professional lobby firm

Our success derives from confidence that we can match promise with performance. Notable specific successes have been achieved. Among them, we have saved the international motor-car and motor cycle industries based in the United Kingdom millions of pounds by persuading the Government to exempt them from the provisions of the Trade Descriptions Act, severely reduced demands on an American company for back-payment of British excise duties, secured British Government planning permission for an oil platform building site.

We normally expect to achieve results without any publicity. But, on occasion, even Ministers and senior officials have asked us to help in creating a particular climate of public opinion to enable them the more easily to assist one of our clients whose case they have accepted.

Source: brochure of Lloyd-Hughes Associates, quoted in *Hansard*, 2.2.82

8.34

Registration of lobbyists

In the United States all 10,000 lobbyists on Capitol Hill must be registered. In Britain no such safeguard exists. Another area of concern is the extraordinary dual role played by several lobbyists who work for business clients and directly for the Government, as contracted advisers. Some firms, like Mr Smith's Political Communication, operate mainly in the purely political sphere. One of his conspicuous successes was to persuade the Environment Secretary, Mr Nicholas Ridley to drop plans for the storage of radioactive waste. Evie Soames, of the public relations firm Charles Barker, ran one campaign on behalf of various unnamed racing interests, which bore fruit in the last budget with the abolition of on-course betting duty.

Source: adapted from David Rose, *Guardian*, 8.1.88

8.35

Estimated turnover of lobby firms

| 1982 | £1m |
| 1987 | £10m |

Source: David Rose, *op. cit.*

8.36

Many MPs and ministers are now anaesthetised to much organisational lobbying. Its effect has been diluted by overuse. The much-vaunted British Airways parliamentary lobby, so carefully and skilfully constructed since 1984, is now so slick that ministers expect it and discount accordingly.

Source: Charles Miller, *Contemporary Record*, Spring 1988

E. Conclusion: are pressure groups harmful or beneficial to democracy?

ACTIVITY 14

A   Using sources 8.37–8.39 as a starting point, construct a case in support of the view that pressure groups are of vital importance to the effective functioning of representative democracy in Britain.

B   Are pressure groups powerful enough? Explain your answer.

C   What criticisms might be made of the theory of pluralism outlined in data 8.37?

8.37

The Pluralist Model

The basic framework of this model is that there is a consensus on the nature of the political system, on the rules of the game, and that the role of government is to act as independent arbiter among the competing demands of groups. Within the political process, the essential element is the group, and the political system is characterized by individuals having the opportunity to join groups, doing so, and then, through these groups, enjoying access to government. Pluralists emphasize the extent and range of groups, their access to government, and the competition between them. There is presumed to be something of a balance among groups, no one group enjoying supremacy, and the balance and institutionalized relationship between groups and government provides for both stability in the political system and incremental policy-making.

Source: Philip Norton, *The British Polity*, Longman, 1984, p. 164

8.38

'People do not join political parties today. If they want something done they're much more likely to join a pressure group.'

Source: Geoffrey Alderman quoted in Davies, *op. cit.*

ACTIVITY 15

How far do you agree with the hypothesis that 'pressure groups are too powerful and are harmful to democracy'? Take into account:

A   Examples of pressure group action which you believe are harmful to democracy.

B   The arguments which explain why pressure groups might be considered over-powerful and harmful to democracy.

C   Pressure groups which you believe should have more influence over government.

8.39

In defence of pressure groups

(1) There is more to democracy than the occasional vote. To be healthy, a democracy needs participation at every level.
(2) Pressure groups offer a chance for minorities and the disadvantaged to argue their case.
(3) Pressure groups improve surveillance of government.
(4) Pressure groups combat other pressure groups.
(5) Pressure groups maintain the momentum and give causes their stamina.
(6) Pressure groups relieve frustration.

Source: adapted from Des Wilson, *Contemporary Record*, Spring 1988

Further reading

Alderman, G., *Pressure Groups and Government in Great Britain*, Longman, 1984

Coxall, W.N., *Parties and Pressure Groups* (2nd edn.), Longman, 1986

Davies, M., *Politics of Pressure*, BBC Publications, 1985

Wilson, D., *Pressure: The A to Z of Campaigning in Britain*, Heinemann, 1984

Contemporary Record, Vol. 2, No. 1, Spring, 1988

UNIT 9 Protest and Dissent

'It is bad when groups of people make disturbances and we do not approve of it. But when disturbances do occur, they force us to learn lessons from them . . . In this sense, bad things can be turned into good things.' (Mao Tse-Tung)

'You may well ask: "Why direct action? Why sit-ins, marches, etc.? Isn't negotiation a better path?''. You are exactly right in your call for negotiation, indeed this is the purpose of direct action . . . It seeks so to dramatise the issue that it can no longer be ignored.' (Martin Luther King)

Introduction

These statements, by two men who had such a huge impact on postwar political developments, encapsulate the arguments for protest and dissent. Politics is about power, and protestors seek to influence the decisions of those with power.

Usually when power is exercised there are winners and losers, and studies of power in communities suggest that some people are consistent beneficiaries of the decision-making process, while others lose most of the time. Protest and dissent are results of the inequalities in the distribution of power and resources.

This unit examines protest and dissent principally in the context of British politics. The conclusions drawn are, however, applicable to any Western democracy.

A. Why obey authority?

The political behaviour of people can vary along a continuum from absolute compliance to complete disobedience. In Britain, most people tend to comply voluntarily with laws and decisions, and even in Northern Ireland, with continuing para-military violence, the majority of citizens obey the law. However, Britain has a long history of political protest and dissent – much of it violent. Protest, including non-violent civil disobedience, continues to be a feature of contemporary British politics, and the 1980s were marked by serious urban unrest.

Why should anyone obey the law? Philosophers have long argued about the basis of political obligation. Some argue that we ought to obey the law because we are **morally** obliged to do so, other say **prudence** dictates that people ought to accept political authority. Arguments such as 'we must obey because it is right and proper' are contrasted with 'we must obey because otherwise society would be chaotic and ungovernable'. Some people argue that citizens accept laws and political decisions either because they are frightened of being punished if they do not, or because of habit and tradition – an unthinking acceptance of political authority.

ACTIVITY 1

A Write a short statement on why you think people obey political decisions and new laws.

B Now write a short statement on whether people **should** obey the law. Can you think of any examples of laws or government actions which you feel should **not** be obeyed? Explain your reasons, and how you think such laws should be resisted.

B. Participation, legitimacy and obedience

Politics involves conflict and disagreement over ideas and interests and the resolution of that conflict through compromise, co-operation or coercion, and as such it entails rules and procedures. Clearly dissent is central to politics, and this dissent may concern the outcomes of decision making or there may be dissent over the decision-making process itself.

Key concepts are **participation** and **legitimacy**. The importance of participation to political systems is widely recognised. In democracies a basic form of participation is elections, which are a vital means of legitimising the regime and of achieving voluntary obedience. Political participation, through institutions such as parties and pressure groups, is one of the chief ways whereby demands are articulated. Participation tends to reinforce citizens' identification with the rules, procedures and values of the system.

Participation is also a source of legitimacy in a democratic society. Essentially, legitimacy is the quality of being lawful or right. A claim that something is legitimate rests upon the assertion that it is proper according to rules or principles, but legitimacy involves more than this – that is compliance with prevailing cultural values.

Both participation and legitimacy are related to **consent**. Citizens are more likely to consent to government decisions about which they have had the opportunity to voice their views, and when there is a high level of legitimacy. Conversely, low levels of participation and legitimacy are likely to generate increased dissent among groups of citizens.

ACTIVITY 2

A Study 9.1. Comment on the view of participation illustrated by this cartoonist.

B What do the charts (9.2) reveal about political participation in Britain? What do they show about political legitimacy and the potential for protest?

C In teams, draw up short questionnaires on the same themes and carry out a simple sample survey in your school or college. What do students think about participation and political action? Analyse and comment on the results (see also, Activity 6).

9.1

'More trouble-makers!'

Attitudes to political participation

How much say do you think you should have about what the Government does?

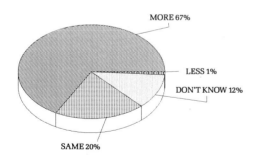

MORE 67%
LESS 1%
DON'T KNOW 12%
SAME 20%

How well does the Government meet the needs of the people?

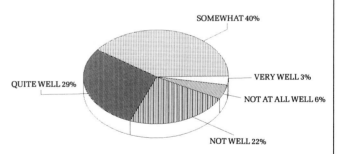

SOMEWHAT 40%
VERY WELL 3%
QUITE WELL 29%
NOT AT ALL WELL 6%
NOT WELL 22%

Is voting the only way a citizen can have a say about how governments work?

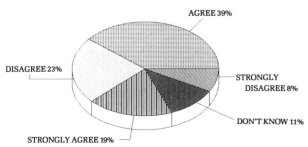

AGREE 39%
DISAGREE 23%
STRONGLY DISAGREE 8%
STRONGLY AGREE 19%
DON'T KNOW 11%

How well prepared are you to participate in political action?

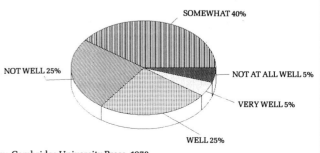

SOMEWHAT 40%
NOT WELL 25%
NOT AT ALL WELL 5%
VERY WELL 5%
WELL 25%

9.2

Source: V. Hart, *Distrust and Democracy*, Cambridge University Press, 1978

ACTIVITY 3
Study data 9.3 and 9.4

A   Consider these statements carefully: what are the central points they are making? Are ideas such as 'loyalty', 'identity' and 'trust' important in politics and in explaining dissent? How do the data in 9.2 relate to these concepts?
B   Make a list of different methods of political participation which a citizen or group might employ to express their dissent. Identify and explain which of the forms of political action on your list can be described as 'protest'.

9.3

The opportunity to participate in political decisions is associated with greater satisfaction with that system and with greater general loyalty . . . the sense of ability to participate in politics appears to increase the legitimacy of a system.

Source: G. Almond and S. Verba, *The Civic Culture: Political Attitudes and Democracy in Five Nations*, Princeton University Press, 1963, p. 253

9.4

In the normal course of events, participation is nice but not indispensable. What is important is the possibility of participation in order to veto developments, to express dissent.

Source: R. Dahrendorf, 'Effectiveness and legitimacy: on the "governability" of democracies', *The Political Quarterly*, Vol 51, 1980, p. 397

C. Protests in history

The relatively ordered years from 1945 to 1980 appear to have given many people a false idea of public disorder in British history. The violent urban riots – Brixton, St Paul's, Toxteth, Handsworth and Tottenham – have therefore stood out as unique occurrences (see data 9.5). The implication that Britain's towns and cities have in the past been characterised by order and tranquility must be contrasted with the evidence from history (see data 9.6).

Over six hundred years ago, in 1381, England was engulfed in protests about the Poll Tax. The reaction to the new tax, coupled with other injustices, resulted in the insurrection known as the Peasants' Revolt, which threatened to topple the Kingdom. In the eighteenth century, civil commotion was a frequent occurrence. The most notable disorders were the anti-Catholic Gordon Riots in June 1780. During the last century, violent disorders included Luddism, the Post-Napoleonic Wars' disturbances, rural riots and the Sunday Trading riots of 1855.

Many of the violent disorders in Britain have been associated with social grievances, unemployment or lack of political representation. In the disturbance in Trafalgar Square on 13 November 1887, police clashed with unemployed people, leaving 3 dead and 200 injured. The periods before and after the First World War were characterised by extensive disorder, over issues such as votes for women, home rule for Ireland and industrial disputes. Despite frequent assertions to the contrary, the 1930s were also years of considerable disorder, as data 9.7 shows.

ACTIVITY 4
Study data 9.5–9.8

A   Draw up a list of the causes and grievances of the protests shown in Tables 9.6 and 9.7.
B   What opportunities did people have to voice their dissent in the past? Compare these with those that people have today.
C   Does the evidence in data 9.6–9.8 support the views of public disorder contained in 9.5?
D   Write a short essay with the title 'There is more violence and protest in Britain than there used to be'. Make use of the data in this chapter.

9.5

Reactions to urban riots in the 1980s

'Alien to our streets.'

Sir Kenneth Newman, Metropolitan Police Commissioner

'The vast majority of people expect the precepts of Anglo-Saxon behaviour and of law and order to be maintained. These standards must be maintained, despite what other ethnic minorities want.'

Sir Peter Emery, MP for Honiton

9.6

Examples of rioting, 1757–1919

1757   Militia Act riots against being balloted for the militia, mainly in Lincolnshire and Yorkshire.

1766   Widespread food riots. Major areas of disturbances in the West Country, Thames Valley, Midlands and East Anglia.

1768   Demonstration in support of John Wilkes in London. 'Massacre' of St George's Fields: some of Wilkes's supporters killed by soldiers when demonstrating outside the King's Bench Prison (May).

1780   Gordon riots in London. Lord George Gordon led the Protestant Association in a campaign to repeal the Catholic Relief Act of 1778. A mass lobby of Parliament to present a petition on 2 June led to almost a week of rioting with attacks on the property of Catholics and prominent public buildings. Newgate prison burned and over 300 people killed or executed as a result of riots.

1794   'Crimp house' riots in London; attacks on recruiting houses for illegally obtaining recruits.

An attack on the workhouse at Stockport, 1842.

1795–6   Widespread food riots following poor harvests in 1794 and 1795.

1811–12   Luddite machine-breaking outbreaks (began March 1811) in Midlands, Yorkshire, Lancashire and Cheshire. Renewed outbreaks occurred in 1814 and 1816.

1816   Widespread disturbances against high prices and unemployment on the conclusion of the Napoleonic Wars. Main centres in East Anglia and manufacturing districts. Spa Fields riot in London. Attack on gunshops and Tower of London by group of revolutionary followers of Thomas Spence.

1819   Reform demonstration broken up at St Peter's Fields, Manchester. Eleven killed and nearly 200 wounded – the 'Peterloo Massacre'.

1826   Power-looms destroyed in Lancashire (April–May).

1830–3   'Captain Swing' disturbances among agricultural districts in southern England. Hundreds of demonstrations, riots, machine-breakings and arson attempts. Several hundred labourers transported. Reform disturbances in London (November 1830).

1842   'Plug-plot' riots and Chartist General Strike in the North and Potteries (July–August).

1887   'Bloody Sunday'; meeting of Social Democratic Federation in Trafalgar Square broken up by police and troops (13 November).

1911   Clashes between police and strikers in Liverpool on 'Bloody Sunday' (13 August) and two strikers shot by troops (15 August). Two men shot at Llanelli (17 August).

1919   Clashes between police and strikers during General Strike in Glasgow, known as 'Bloody Friday' (31 June). Troops called to patrol city. Demobilisation disturbances in London and at Rhyl, North Wales (March). Police strike in Liverpool followed by rioting in central districts (August).

Source: adapted from C. Cook and J. Stevenson, *Longman Handbook of Modern History*, Longman, 1983

9.7

1931

Jan: At Highbury, crowds sweep police aside.

Mar: Crime wave reported.

Jun: Gang disorder in London.

Jul: Orange riots in Liverpool (50 hurt).

Aug: Street battle in Oxford; riot in Manchester: 1000 fight police.

Sep: Clashes between police and Welsh hunger marchers at Trades Union Congress in Bristol; police baton unemployed marchers in Whitehall; violence between unemployed and police in Dundee, Birmingham, Glasgow, and Manchester; Royal Navy mutiny at Invergordon; trouble in Liverpool.

Oct: Mounted police charge unemployed in Salford; more rioting in Glasgow; 80,000 unemployed march in Manchester; police turn fire hoses on them; many people clubbed by police; violent clashes between police and unemployed in London, Blackburn and Cardiff; riot at Moseley meeting in Birmingham; trouble at Leicester meeting; more disturbances in London and Cardiff; National Government under MacDonald elected.

Nov: Disorder in Shoreditch, elsewhere in London and in Coventry; marches and demonstrations against the means test.

Dec: Police and unemployed clash in Liverpool, Wallsend, London, Leeds, Glasgow, Wigan, Kirkcaldy, Stoke-on-Trent and elsewhere.

Source: J. Benyon and J. Solomos, *The Roots of Urban Unrest*, Pergamon, 1987

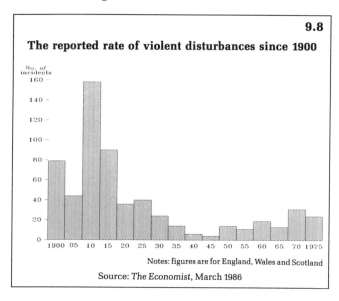

9.8

The reported rate of violent disturbances since 1900

No. of incidents

Notes: figures are for England, Wales and Scotland

Source: *The Economist*, March 1986

The Suffragettes

One of the greatest protest movements of this century was that of the Suffragettes. Founded in 1903 by Christabel Pankhurst and her mother Emmeline, the Women's Social and Political Union (WSPU) took up the argument that women should have a vote. Data 9.9 outlines the development of the movement, while data 9.10–9.11 illustrate some of the tactics which they used.

ACTIVITY 5
Study data 9.9–9.13

A List the methods of protest which the Suffragettes employed. Were there any of which you disapprove – and if so, why? Do you think they might have used different forms of protest with more effect?

B In what ways do data 9.12 and 9.13 differ in their interpretations of the Suffragette's actions? How do you explain this difference?

9.9

The Suffragette Movement

Mid 19th century	– John Stuart Mill and others argued that women should have a vote.
1903	– WSPU founded.
1906	– Liberal government elected. Politicians such as Asquith heckled; marches and demonstrations were organised.
1907	– Movement divided. Some left WSPU to form the Women's Freedom League (WFL). Bigger demonstrations in Hyde Park. Members of WFL chained themselves to railings at the House of Commons.
1909	– Imprisoned women began hunger strikes and were force-fed.
1912	– WSPU adopted more militant tactics which included smashing windows and more marches.
1913	– Emily Davison threw herself under the King's horse at the Derby; her funeral was an enormous demonstration in favour of the cause. Houses were set on fire, telegraph wires were cut and paintings were slashed.
1914	– Prime Minister Asquith met a deputation and it seemed that votes for women would become a reality but war intervened.
1918	– Women over thirty received the vote, partly in recognition of the role played by women in the war.
1928	– Women became entitled to vote on the same basis as men at age 21.

9.10

9.11

9.12

SHE. IT IS TIME I GOT OUT OF THIS PLACE.
WHERE SHALL I FIND THE KEY?

CONVICTS
AND
LUNATICS
HAVE NO VOTE
FOR
PARLIAMENT

9.13

I break the law from no selfish motive. I have no
personal end to serve, neither have any of the other
women who have gone through this court during the
past few weeks, like sheep to the slaughter. Not one of
these women would, if women were free, be law-
breakers. They are women who seriously believe that
this hard path that they are treading is the only path to
their enfranchisement.

Source: Emmeline Pankhurst, *My Own Story*, Virago, 1979 (First published
1914)

D. Different types of protest

Protest and dissent may take a number of different forms. Table 9.14 gives one analysis of 'unorthodox political
behaviour' and examines popular support for each.

ACTIVITY 6
Study data 9.14

A   What conclusions do you draw from this table
about popular attitudes to different types of
protest?
B   Compare this table with the evidence from history
offered by 9.6. What differences and similarities
are there? Do you think that there has been a
change of attitude toward types of protest over the
years?
C   Which of these activities would you be prepared
to engage in? Include this question in the sample
survey suggested in Activity 2. How do your
fellow students' views compare with the data in
9.14? Account for any differences.

9.14

The limits of support for unorthodox political behaviour

	APPROVE OF %	BELIEVE EFFECTIVE %	HAVE DONE %
Sign petitions	86	73	23
Lawful demonstrations	69	60	6
Boycotts	37	48	6
Rent strikes	24	27	2
Unofficial strikes	16	42	5
Occupying buildings	15	29	1
Blocking traffic	15	31	1
Painting slogans on walls	1	6	–
Damaging property	2	10	1
Personal violence	2	11	–

Source: Alan Marsh, *Protest and Political Consciousness*, London, Sage
Publications, 1977

Demonstrations

As the quote by Martin Luther King at the beginning of this chapter makes clear, the principal purposes of protest are first to direct attention to the particular issue, and second to force those with power – the decision makers – to begin negotiations.

One of the most common methods of protest is to organise a demonstration – to 'demonstrate' opposition and strength of feeling for or against a proposal. But marches and demonstrations (which may be static meetings – not marches) may cause great inconvenience to other people and they are very expensive to police. Violence and other criminal activity may occur at large protest gatherings. Some marches may be provocative and deeply upsetting to other people.

ACTIVITY 7
Study data 9.15–9.17

A   Do you think marches and demonstrations should be allowed – are they necessary in a democratic society?
B   Draw up a list of matters about which you would be prepared to go on a demonstration.
C   Are there particular sorts of demonstrations which you think should be banned? Look at the three photographs (9.15–9.17) – would you ban any of them, and if so, why? What are the problems of banning certain sorts of protest?

9.15

9.16

9.17

Civil Disobedience

Dissent and protest may be expressed through the refusal to obey or conform to laws. The precise definition of this type of activity is not easy to arrive at (see data 9.18–9.19). The introduction of the Community Charge in Scotland in 1989 led some members of the public to refuse to make their payment. The justification for such behaviour is offered in data 9.20.

ACTIVITY 8
Study data 9.18–9.20

A What are the similarities and differences between the two definitions of civil disobedience (9.18–9.19)? Which do you think is the most appropriate? Why?

B Write two pieces:
  (i) justifying, and
  (ii) condemning
  Rob Edwards' action (9.20).

C Which of the two definitions in 9.18–9.19 best applies to non-payment of the Community Charge? Explain your answer.

9.18

Civil disobedience 1

Anyone commits an act of civil disobedience if and only if he acts illegally, publicly, nonviolently, and conscientiously with the intent to frustrate (one of) the laws, policies, or decisions of his government.

Source: H. A. Bedau, 'On Civil Disobedience', *Journal of Philosophy*, 1961, p. 661

9.19

Civil disobedience 2

... civil disobedience [is] ... the right, under principles of natural law, to determine which laws are just and to disobey unjust laws provided the disobedience is open and peaceable.

Source: L. F. Powell, 'A Lawyer Looks at Civil Disobedience', *Washington and Lee Law Review*, 1966, p. 343

9.20

When Democracy's All Through

I have decided not to pay the poll tax ... This does not mean that I will go to prison. I will not be guilty of any criminal offence. I will simply put the money aside and wait for Lothian Regional Council to pursue me for debt ... One way or another, it is bound to end up getting the money. I will probably pay a financial penalty – at least 10% on top of my poll tax bill ... so what is the point?

The point first of all, is democracy – the rule of the people. At the last general election, three quarters of the people who voted in Scotland supported political parties who opposed the poll tax ... Scotland has not given its consent to Mrs Thatcher's right to govern ...

The point, too, is the iniquity of the tax itself. Instead of the rates, a crudely redistributive form of property tax, people are going to be taxed simply for existing....

But I still don't think there is any real choice over what to do. Every other avenue of protest has been well traversed. Parliamentary opposition, petitions, propaganda campaigns, public demonstrations – they have all been tried ... As a result, people feel helpless, insubstantial and deprived of power. A non-payment campaign is not in itself going to bring the return of power, but it might help re-establish a little dignity....

Source: Rob Edwards, *New Statesman and Society*, Spring 1989

Riots – Are they protest?

The resurgence of street rioting in the 1980s has raised a number of issues. Each incident has occurred in an inner city area where there is deprivation, where there are significant ethnic populations and where there have been persistent complaints about the police. Do the actions of the participants constitute protest? Considering the causes of these disturbances may shed some light on this question (9.21).

ACTIVITY 9
Study data 9.21

A According to this table, what percentage of respondents perceived the causes of disturbance as 'political/social protest'?

B What other headings might you also consider to be kinds of political and social protest? Why do you think they are listed separately?

C What significance do you attach to the statement that these are 'perceived' causes of local disturbance?

D In what ways could 9.22–9.23 be used to help interpret table 9.21?

E Consider the views in 9.23. How far do you agree with the statement that 'riots are a form of social/political protest'?

9.21

Survey of local people in Handsworth, 1981

Perceived causes of the local disturbances

CAUSES	%
Unemployment	43
Copying other areas	23
Boredom	22
Agitators/political activists	14
Racial tension/discrimination	10
Police harassment	9
Hooliganism	5
Poverty/inflation	4
Poor facilities of the area	3
Lack of parental or school discipline	3
Poor housing	2
Political/social protest	2
Build up of tension/rumours	2
Excuse for looting	2
General atmosphere of country	1
Noisy parties	1
All respondents	(N = 532)

Note: Respondents could choose more than one reason

Source: S. Field and P. Southgate, *Public Disorder*, HMSO, 1982, p. 49

9.22

9.23

Interpreting riots

'...is it not grossly wrong and unfair to talk about social protest? What we should be talking about is sheer criminality.'

David Mellor, Conservative MP

'...those who feel rejected by society will tend to reject the rules of that society.'

Jonathan Sayeed, Conservative MP

'...many of them, it is obvious, believe with justification that violence, though wrong, is a very effective means of protest...'

Lord Scarman

E. Violence – is it ever justified?

Urban riots have once again raised **violent** protest as an issue in mainland Britain. Violence has been a feature of protest in the past (9.6) and in other parts of the world including Northern Ireland (9.24–9.26). But is violence ever justified? This question is considered by John Hoffman (9.25).

ACTIVITY 10
Study data 9.24–9.26

A Using data 9.24 and 9.26 and your general knowledge, would you say that violent protest is widespread? Justify your answer.

B Using data in this chapter, draw up a list of the causes of protest.

C Construct an argument
(i) for, and
(ii) against
the use of violence in protest (9.25).

D Taking the three contemporary cases (9.26), assess the justification for the use of violence in each. Do you support the use of violent protest in any instance?

9.24

50,000 in Titograd protest

Sri Lanka opposition claims fraud at polls and threatens action in streets

Bhutto faces crisis as row erupts over Baluchistan

Tibetans on rights march in Peking

Czech clamp on protests

Language dispute in Quebec raises spectre of violence

9.25

Is Political Violence Ever Justified?

Conventional wisdom has it that violence is evil. Decent people should settle their differences peacefully through discussion and debate. Resorting to the bullet and the bomb is a threat to civilisation and a free society...

Yet once we begin to consider how we might reverse what seems to be a rising tide of menacing violence, we come face-to-face with...

AN UNPALATABLE PARADOX

Anyone who has had to confront a thug or a bully knows that it is impossible to restrain violent people in a purely peaceful way. Invariably it takes force to prevent force...

It is true that under certain circumstances peaceful opposition may stop aggressors in their tracks. But what are these circumstances? They are situations in which aggressor and victim share some kind of common code of ethics so that moral pressure alone serves to shame the aggressor into desisting from further acts of violence...(but) it would seem that in most circumstances the only way to tackle violence is through a willingness and readiness to employ force. The very existence of the state with its police and prisons, its armies and weapons of war testifies to this point...But how can we justify using violence without, at the same time, hopelessly compromising our (wholly legitimate) abhorrence for violence?

There is only one answer. *By using force in such a way and only in such a way that it works to eradicate force...*

An orderly society implies a common interest – a capacity to identify sympathetically with your fellows. Privilege and exploitation...an arrogant belief in the superiority of the male sex or white race; a deepening gulf between the 'haves' and 'have-nots': it is here that the roots of violence surely lie...every moral and political philosopher through the ages has had to acknowledge in one way or another that violence arises through *division*; a divisiveness which strains relationships and destroys community. Once we become conscious of the relationship between violence and division, then it becomes self-evident that the problem of violence must be identified in broad social – as well as narrow political – terms. The conscious violence of the state and the brigand must be linked to the 'unconscious' violence of poverty, disease, destitution and discrimination. Anything which deepens division, creates violence: anything which overcomes division, helps to eradicate violence.

Source: John Hoffman, *Social Studies Review*, November 1988, pp. 61–62

9.26

Political Violence: Three Contemporary Cases

Violence occurs all over the world, in and between various countries, perpetrated by quite disparate states and groups, and involving very different aims and demands. Here are three examples of groups involved in political violence.

The African National Congress of South Africa (ANC) – Formed in 1912 but only resorted to armed struggle in the 1960s after all constitutional channels of opposition were finally closed. Seeks to avoid civilian casualties and to unite the widest possible coalition of forces inside and outside South Africa in the struggle against apartheid.

The Provisional Irish Republican Army (PIRA) – Formed in late 1969 as a breakaway from the IRA, in the wake of attacks on the Catholic community in Northern Ireland by loyalist mobs, who were helped rather than hindered by the police of the day. Expresses the frustration of those who feel that constitutional democracy is impossible in a six-county Ulster with its (contrived) Unionist majority. Embraces a strategy of violence which appears indiscriminate and has deeply divided Irish democrats north as well as south of the border.

The Red Brigades in Italy; Baader Meinhof in West Germany – One of the most extreme by-products of the student rebellions in the 1960s. Sees the liberal parliamentary system as a positive barrier to social progress and hence employs force as a way of provoking an authoritarian response from the state. It believes that in this way a dedicated elite can awaken opposition to 'the system' from an otherwise duped and misguided majority.

Source: *Social Studies Review*, November 1988, p. 62

F. Conclusion

Public concern about the perceived rising tide of violent protest has led to recent legislation. The Public Order Act of 1986 (9.27) attempts to balance the rights of the individual not to be inconvenienced with the rights of the protestor. There is disagreement as to whether it succeeds in this task (9.29–9.30).

In the final analysis, decisions are about power. Inevitably, those who do not benefit from the exercise of power are likely to express dissent. On occasions this dissent will be manifest as angry protest. Perhaps the most surprising aspect of politics is that the losers do not protest more often.

ACTIVITY 11
Study data 9.27–9.30

A   In what ways does the Public Order Act, 1986, (9.27) seek to achieve the compromise described by Lord Scarman (9.28)?
B   How do the writers of 9.29 and 9.30 disagree about the prospects for the Public Order Act?
C   Do you think it is surprising that there is not **more** dissent and protest in Britain?

9.27

Summary of the Public Order Act 1986

(1)   It makes it a national requirement to give seven days notice to the police of any march or procession. Failure to do this will constitute an offence.
(2)   The police are given the power to ban single marches on grounds of the apprehension of serious public disorder.
(3)   It is made a criminal offence to participate in a prohibited march.
(4)   The police are given the power to impose conditions either in advance, or on the spot, on the grounds that they are necessary to prevent disruption of the community or coercion of individuals, as well as on the grounds of the apprehension of serious public disorder.
(5)   The police may impose conditions concerning the location, number of participants and duration of any open air or static demonstration.
(6)   A range of offences is created including disorderly conduct, threatening behaviour, affray, violent disorder and riot.

9.28

Amongst our fundamental human rights there are, without doubt, the rights of peaceful assembly and public protest, and the right to public order and tranquility. Civilised living collapses – it is obvious – if public protest becomes violent protest or public order degenerates into the quietism imposed by successful oppression. But the problem is more complex than a choice between two extremes – one, a right to protest whenever and wherever you will, and the other, a right to continuous calm upon our streets unruffled by the noise and obstructive pressure of the protesting procession. A balance has to be struck, a compromise found, that will accommodate the exercise of the right to protest within a framework of public order which enables ordinary citizens, who are not protesting, to go about their business and pleasure without obstruction or inconvenience. The fact that those who at any one time are concerned to secure the tranquility of the streets are likely to be the majority must not lead us to deny the protesters their opportunity to march: the fact that the protesters are desperately sincere and are exercising a fundamental human right must not lead us to overlook the rights of the majority.

Source: Lord Scarman, *Report on the Inquiry into the Red Lion Square Disorders*, (Cmnd 5919), HMSO, 1974

9.29

Public Order Act: Verdict 1

These powers mean that the police will be able to decide whether crowds of every kind can gather ... they will make protesting citizens into licensed visitors to their own streets.

Source: *Guardian*, 7.12.85

9.30

Public Order Act: Verdict 2

It seems ... as though the right of the individual not to be interfered with is now perceived as of greater importance than the right of protest or freedom of assembly.

Source: *New Law Journal*, 24.5.85

Further reading

Benyon, J. and Solomos, J. (eds) *The Roots of Urban Unrest*, Oxford: Pergamon Press, 1987
Murphy, J. G. (ed) *Civil Disobedience and Violence*, Belmont, California: Wadsworth, 1971
Pearson, G. *Hooligan: A History of Respectable Fears*, London: Macmillan, 1983
Pryce, K. *Endless Pressure*, Harmondsworth: Penguin, 1979
Quinault, R. and Stevenson, J. *Popular Protest and Public Order*, London: Allen and Unwin, 1977
Wilson, D. *Citizen Action*, Harlow: Longman, 1986

UNIT 10
The Politics of Nuclear Power

The task set by this unit is to look at how the issue of nuclear energy affects British politics, and in turn how some of Britain's political institutions and processes have affected the nuclear energy debate.

Introduction

We often take energy for granted. But it is essential for modern manufacturing, domestic and transport purposes. The oil crises of 1973–4 and 1979–80 caused havoc around the world and led to very damaging economic recessions.

Those who argue for building **more nuclear power** stations (currently nuclear energy supplies 20 per cent of the UK's electricity generation), say that as the world's demands for energy continues to grow, nuclear power will be needed to replace diminishing reserves of fossil fuels (coal, oil and gas). Other 'renewable' sources of energy (eg wind, wave, solar, tidal, geothermal power and biofuels), will take time to develop.

More recently, advocates of nuclear power have said we need more nuclear power and less fossil fuels because the carbon dioxide, given off when fossil fuels are burned, heats up the planet leading to changing climates and rising sea levels. This is known as the 'greenhouse effect'. **Opponents of nuclear power** say that radioactive nuclear waste from power stations cannot be safely disposed of. They say that nuclear power stations are unsafe, citing the USA's Three Mile Island and the USSR's Chernobyl accidents as examples. They also fear that nuclear power means more centralisation and authoritarian security measures to protect it. It is also claimed that civil nuclear power assists the spread of nuclear weapons.

Anti-nuclear campaigners say that we can meet our future energy demands and reduce reliance on fossil fuels first by cutting our wasteful energy uses (energy conservation) and second by investing in renewable sources of energy rather than nuclear power.

A. Energy as a political issue

ACTIVITY 1
Study data 10.1–10.3

A Why do you think energy is such an important political issue?

B Explain the dilemma which faces anti-nuclear campaigners as a result of the 'greenhouse effect'.

C The Green Party says that we could reduce the pollution energy causes by producing fewer goods and restricting economic growth. Discuss whether this is a realistic strategy.

D To what extent do the figures in 10.3 demonstrate that nuclear energy is principally a political rather than an economic issue?

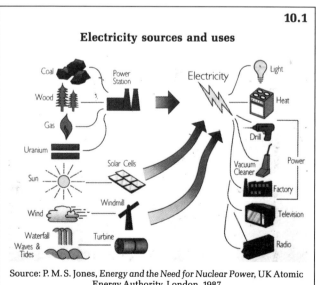

10.1

Electricity sources and uses

Source: P. M. S. Jones, *Energy and the Need for Nuclear Power*, UK Atomic Energy Authority, London, 1987

The Greenhouse Effect

10.2

Source: Earth Action Report, No. 3 Dec/Jan 1988/89

10.3

Comparison of costs of electricity from Hinkley Point B (nuclear) and Drax (coal fired) power stations.

	HINKLEY POINT B p/kWh[1]	DRAX (FIRST HALF) p/kWh
	1983/4	1983/4
Capital[2] Costs	1.37	0.47
Fuel Costs	0.93	1.81
Other costs	0.34	0.18
	2.64	2.46

1 Pence per kilowatt/hour
2 Costs of building the power stations

Source: Analysis of generation costs, CEGB, 1984

B. Party attitudes and public opinion

The accident in Chernobyl in April 1986 did have an impact upon public opinion and influenced the discussions at the Labour and Liberal Party Conferences that autumn.

Each of the parties adopted policy positions on the issue of nuclear energy during the 1987 General Election campaign. The Conservative Party pursued a policy of developing nuclear power (10.4), while Labour committed itself to a gradual phase-out. The Alliance was divided on the issue.

Shifting public opinion is only one of the factors which influences party politics. Often the concerns of special interest groups such as the trade unions, which control five-sixths of Labour Conference votes, or security concerns, as in the case of the Conservative Party, are of greater importance in deciding policy stances. The influence of public opinion on party policies can be compared with some of the other factors.

ACTIVITY 2
Study Data 10.4 to 10.8

A　Comment on the different impacts that changes in public opinion seem to have on opposition party policies compared with those of the party in government.

B　In what ways do the trade unions influence (i) the Labour Party, and (ii) the Conservative Party over the nuclear energy issue?

C　Which manifesto policy appears closest to 'public opinion' at the time of the June 1987 General Election? (See data 10.8)

D　Which manifesto policy would you have supported? What is the salience (relative importance) of nuclear power as an issue in your mind compared with other important issues? To help you answer this, construct a list of six policy areas that are most important to you and place them in rank order. Where, if anywhere, does nuclear energy occur?

10.4

Conservative policy 1987

A commitment to go on playing a leading role in the task of developing abundant, low cost supplies of nuclear electricity and managing the associated waste products.

Source: Conservative Party Manifesto, 1987

10.5

Alliance policy 1987

Existing capacity and planned coal-fired power stations are enough to meet our needs for some time to come and *we see no case for proceding with a PWR at Sizewell or other nuclear power stations at the present time.* Safety must come first and after Chernobyl there is clearly a need for wider investigation into the safety of nuclear power, and there is also a need for a thorough and independent review of the economics of nuclear power generation.

We will continue research into nuclear fission power including research into the fast breeder reactor which may be needed if renewable resources prove to be less viable than we believe.

Source: SDP/Liberal Alliance election manifesto, 1987

10.6

Labour policy 1987

As the 1987 General Election drew closer, the Labour Leadership's commitment to the Conference Policy of phasing out nuclear power began to weaken, in part, presumably because the energy issue did not seem, as had at one time been expected, to be likely to be a major election focus. Labour's Manifesto simply talked of 'gradually diminishing dependence' on nuclear power...

...in the event, the nuclear issue did not feature significantly in the election. (The Alliance was somewhat split on the issue, the Liberals having a long-standing anti-nuclear policy, the SDP being ambivalent if not pro.)

Subsequently, some of the key unions that had supported the anti-nuclear position, like the TGWU, began to waver under the impact of strong pressure of the pro-nuclear camp, and from some of their own members in the nuclear industry.

Source: D. Elliot, *Nuclear Power and the UK Trade Union and Labour Movement*, Open University Technology Policy Group, 17, October 1988

10.7

Of more than symbolic importance was Margaret Thatcher's visit to France, as one of her first acts as Prime Minister. The French nuclear programme, based on PWRs, was quoted time and time again in Whitehall and elsewhere as an example of what Britain should be aiming at....

...On Tuesday, 23 October 1979, a Cabinet meeting was held that discussed nuclear power. According to the minutes, the Secretary of State for Energy, David Howell, outlined a substantial programme of thermal reactors totalling some 15 gigawatts of capacity, or ten power stations...It was noted that the strategy would not diminish the requirement for coal, but 'a nuclear programme would have the advantage of removing a substantial proportion of electricity production from the dangers of disruption by industrial action by coal miners or transport workers.' Quite clearly, an attempt was being made to learn some lessons from the coal strikes of the mid-seventies.

Source: Tony Hall, *Nuclear Politics*, Penguin, Harmondsworth 1986, pp. 172–3

10.8

Trends in public attitudes to nuclear power in Britain 1979–1987

Q. "At present, about 20 per cent of the total electricity in Great Britain comes from nuclear power. What do you think should be the development of nuclear power generation in this country?" (* 1987 version. Earlier surveys quoted the then current % contribution from nuclear power.)

A. "They should increase nuclear power generation"
"They should not develop any more at present"
"They should stop generating nuclear power"

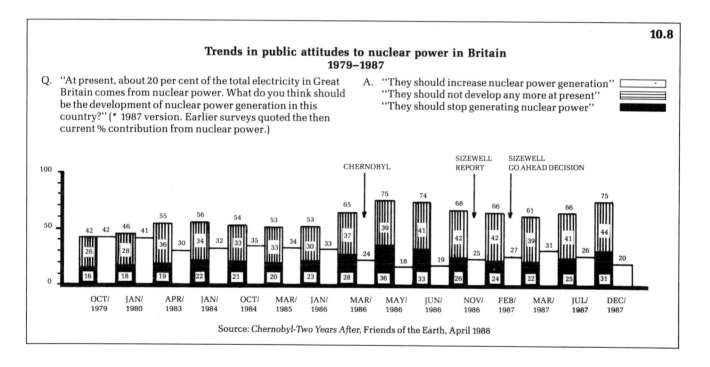

Source: *Chernobyl-Two Years After*, Friends of the Earth, April 1988

C. Nuclear power and ideology in British politics

An ideology is a set of beliefs that are interrelated, a general overview. For instance, left wing socialists in the Labour Party have been less keen on possession of nuclear weapons than the more nationalistic Conservative Party. This section looks at how the issue of nuclear power fits into the left/right ideological debate.

After the nuclear bombing of Japan in 1945, the scientists who had made the bomb wanted to turn this terrible weapon into positive help for mankind through civil nuclear power. The idea of 'Atoms for Peace' was widely supported. But in the 1970s opposition to civil nuclear power grew.

Leftwing opinion had always opposed British possession of nuclear weapons. When evidence emerged that plutonium produced by civil nuclear reactors might have been used in nuclear weapons, anti-nuclear campaigners proclaimed that civil and military nuclear activities were links in the same chain (see 10.10).

Although the material for nuclear weapons can come from sources other than civil nuclear reactors, for many leftwingers the link suggested that nuclear power was merely a cover for the weapons programme. This argument has little impact on those on the right, centre or moderate left who support some sort of UK nuclear deterrent. Some on the right even see the anti-nuclear campaign as a conscious or unconscious attempt to undermine the West in favour of Soviet Communism (see 10.11).

ACTIVITY 3
Study the background information and data
10.9–10.13

A   Do you think that the left is being hypocritical by opposing nuclear weapons and nuclear power in Britain when the Soviet Union has plenty of both? Justify your reply.

B   Describe in your own words the gist of Hoyle's argument (10.11). Do you think he is being fair?

C   Describe the factors, in order of importance, that have influenced your attitude to nuclear power.

D   What does data 10.12 say about the attitude of the anti-nuclear movement to the 'establishment'? How important an influence is the nuclear weapons issue in determining your views on nuclear power?

E   Which, if either, of these two statements do you think is true?
  (i)   a person's attitude to nuclear power is largely determined by whether they are sympathetic to the left or, alternatively, the right;
  (ii) whether someone identifies with the left or the right is largely determined by their attitude to nuclear power.
  Explain your answer.

F   (i)   Make a rough copy of the diagram (10.9) which shows the range of views on public ownership and nuclear weapons. Using the information on party policies given in the previous section, attempt to sketch in the range of views on nuclear power.
  (ii) Now read 10.13. Bearing in mind that the author is opposed to both nuclear power and the possession of nuclear weapons, comment on the usefulness of the left/right axis in defining people's ideological positions. Try to develop a better alternative.

10.9

An approximate* left/right ideological spectrum

Abolish/Reduce	Maintain/Strengthen
NUCLEAR DETERRENT	

More Public Ownership	More Privatisation

LEFT	RIGHT

LABOUR	SLDP/SDP	CONSERVATIVES

* there are some politicians who do not fit in exactly with this model, eg unilateralist SLDP supporters.

10.10

Bomb factories

Nuclear reactors were originally designed to produce plutonium for nuclear weapons. They were and are bomb factories. Their economic viability depends more on the generation of plutonium than electricity. Perhaps this explains the insistence of politicians and the industry on its cheapness against all the evidence. They also maintain the total separation between civil and nuclear use. Yet recent information has revealed that in British plants plutonium passes from Britain to the US military and from civil to military hands and back again.

Source: Jenny Hammond, Critical Mess, Links 26, Third World First, Oxford, 1986

Inspired by the Kremlin   **10.11**

... I have myself welcomed the concern now felt by many people for saving birds, trees, natural beauty, the whale and the Atlantic salmon. It is unfortunately the case that there are always ... political animals who manipulate such movements for their own ends ...

I believe the motive (for this manipulation) to be connected with the Soviet Union, and with a world struggle for energy ...

If you were Russian, you would surely take careful note of that great crescent containing nearly 70 per cent of world oil reserves which starts in the USSR and sweeps through the Middle East into North Africa ...

Believing in the all-importance of energy you would scent victory in the world struggle ... The fly in this otherwise smooth ointment, which in your Russian guise you have prepared, is nuclear energy.

... Evidently then you start your vociferous friends in the West baying against nuclear energy. You instruct your friends to operate through a mild, pleasant, 'save the animals' movement which you observe to be growing popular throughout the western democracies. And all this they do, right to the last letter of your Kremlin-inspired instructions.

Source: Fred Hoyle, Energy or Extinction, Heineman, London, 1979

10.12

Source: Rob Edwards, The Plutonium Connection, CND, 1983

10.13

...let me speak as an out-and-out Green. Not a socialist green, nor a liberal green, nor a green growthist. As such I don't much care to be told that the Democrats or the Labour Party, or some kind of reformed, mud-green version of industrialism are essential to the future of green politics. In reality they remain highly prejudicial to that future. I say that partly on ideological grounds (though I do not happen to believe that the exquisite refining of a comprehensive green ideology is either necessary or desirable), but largely because the collective vision underpinning these different ideologies is itself unsustainable.

Source: Jonathon Porritt in Felix Dodds (ed), *Into the 21st Century*, Greenprint, Basingstoke, 1988

D. Nuclear power and pressure-group politics

Pressure groups differ from political parties in that they do not themselves compete for political office, but try to influence policy decisions. Differentiating between **cause** and **interest** groups (10.14) can be useful in understanding the impact that pressure groups may have on a policy area.

ACTIVITY 4

A List (i) the cause groups, and (ii) the interest groups mentioned in data 10.14, 10.15, 10.16 and 10.19.
B How do the types of arguments about nuclear power used by cause groups differ from those deployed by interest groups? (see data 10.15 and 10.16).
C What trades union interests might have persuaded Arthur Scargill to oppose nuclear power? (10.16).

10.14

Cause and interest groups

...First there are the promotional or attitude groups. These promote a cause, and their potential membership is in theory coextensive with the entire population. Among such groups are the Campaign for Nuclear Disarmament, the Abortion Law Reform Association, the Society for the Protection of the Unborn Child...

Second there are the interest groups like trade unions and business groups, and these are usually based on occupation or economic interest. The distinction between the two groups is not always clearcut. Some *cause* groups may have self-interested supporters... and interest groups try as a rule to identify their campaign with a wider *cause* (as does the National Union of Mineworkers in promoting coal as the major form of energy). Because *cause* groups have so few tangible rewards to offer their supporters, and so few sanctions to wield, they appear to be weaker than interest groups.

Source: D. Kavanagh, *British Politics; Continuities and Change*, Oxford, 1985

10.15

The environmentalists

The environmentalists are a coalition of groups like Greenpeace, Friends of the Earth, the Scottish Campaign to Resist the Atomic Menace (SCRAM) and the Socialist Environment and Resources Association. They attack nuclear power in general and reprocessing in particular. They lack a coherent viewpoint, but their general argument is that large projects like nuclear power stations are examples of *big* or *hard* technology that are not in harmony with the environment, that they are wasteful in resource terms and dangerous and destructive to the environment...

Source: Andrew Massey, The Politics of Nuclear Energy, *Social Studies Review* Vol 1 No. 5 May 1986

10.16

Scargill demand to end nuclear power rejected

The Trades Union Congress overwhelmingly rejected a call yesterday from Mr Arthur Scargill, the miners' leader, for an end to nuclear power in Britain. He said... 'The CEGB had deliberately lied to the people over the years. They had said that nuclear – powered – generated electricity was cheaper than coal. They had now conceded that coal fired generation was considerably cheaper...'

Mr Bill McCall, General Secretary of the Institute of Professional Civil Servants said... 'The closure of all nuclear plants would lead to between 10,000 and 100,000 people losing their jobs. Whole communities would be destroyed where unemployment was already high. Closure would lead to a shortfall in energy, further unemployment and at least a 15 per cent increase in electricity prices...'

Source: *The Times*, 11.9.87

Another method of categorising pressure groups is by looking at their relationship with government. **Insider groups** will concentrate on influencing the government through links with civil servants and Ministers, while **outsider groups** will aim chiefly to influence public opinion. Some outsider groups will even break the law to attract attention.

ACTIVITY 5

A   Write down, as headings, the six categories of pressure groups suggested in data 10.17 and enter all the pressure groups mentioned in data 10.14–10.19 under the headings that you think are the most appropriate for each one.

B   Comment on the relative strengths of the pro- and anti-nuclear camps among (i) cause groups, (ii) interest groups, (iii) insider groups and (iv) outsider groups.

C   Read data 10.18 and explain the difficulties encountered by Friends of the Earth in seeking insider status.

D   Which of the two methods of analysing pressure groups outlined in this section do you think is most useful for studying pressure group activity on the nuclear power issue? Justify your answer.

10.18

Cooperation or confrontation

...the greatest dilemma facing FOE [Friends of the Earth] is whether to cooperate or confront. To the extent to which direct access and incorporation have been obtained, FOE has had to moderate the excesses of its media stunts and FOE Ltd has lost the support of activists in FOE local groups. Direct incorporation into policy-making committees has been infrequent – the only examples being bottle recycling and waste management, both of which were unsuccessful. But FOE Ltd has obviously thought it could gain from participation...

Source: A. R. Ball and F. Millard (ed), *Pressure Group Politics in Industrial Societies*, Macmillan, Basingstoke, 1986, p. 193

10.19

A powerful coalition

Most observers agree that nuclear power politics have been dominated by a powerful coalition of state and private sector concerns in alliance with parts of bureaucracy... In the state sector, the main actors involved include the Central Electricity Generating Board (CEGB), the largest nationalised industry and overseer of the largest integrated grid system outside the USSR, and the UK Atomic Energy Authority which oversees both civil and military nuclear research. The major firms in the private sector include GEC, now Britain's largest industrial firm, Northern Engineering Industries, and large construction companies such as Taylor Woodrow. Not only national capital is involved in the industry. Westinghouse, the American multinational, will supply technology and critical parts for the proposed Sizewell reactor, while Rio Tinto Zinc dominates British Uranium supplies. The point to be noted is that the anti-nuclear movement faces extremely powerful economic interest.

Source: Alan R. Ball and Francis Millard, *op. cit.*, p. 195

10.17

Insider and outsider groups

Insider groups may be subdivided into three categories: *prisoner* groups, *low-profile* insider groups; and *high-profile* insider groups. *Prisoner* groups are those groups which find it particularly difficult to break away from an insider relationship with government either because they are dependent on government for assistance of various kinds – for example the loan of staff or provision of office accommodation – or because they represent parts of the public sector...

The distinction between a *low-profile* and a *high-profile* insider group depends upon the extent to which the pressure group puts itself in the public eye through the use of the media...

Potential insider groups are a transitional category. They would like to become insider groups but face the problem of gaining government's attention as a prelude to their being accepted as groups which should be consulted in relation to particular policy areas....

Outsider groups by necessity may also wish to become insider groups. However, they may lack political sophistication in the sense of an understanding of the way in which the political system works and the importance of gaining access to civil servants...

Ideological outsider groups are careful not to become too closely entangled with the political-administrative system because they wish to challenge accepted authority and institutions. Rather than become an accepted part of the existing system, they wish to replace it or alter it in some fundamental way.

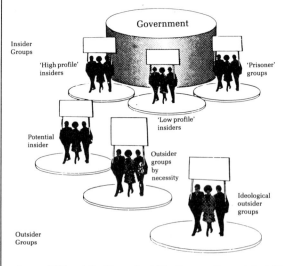

Source: W. Grant, 'Insider and outsider Pressure Groups', *Social Studies Review*, Vol 1 No 1, 1985

E. Protest, dissent and public relations

A progaganda war is being waged by both pro- and anti-nuclear forces. What sort of tactics do they use to gain public attention?

ACTIVITY 6

A Compare the contrasting images of nuclear power put forward by BNFL (10.20) and anti-nuclear protestors in 10.24. Which, in your opinion, is more accurate?

B List the different tactics employed by anti-nuclear protestors in data 10.21–10.24 in order of their degree of confrontation with the state. Say whether each tactic in the list is (i) legal or illegal, (ii) violent or non-violent.

C Why does the nuclear industry feel the need for public relations exercises? (See data 10.20).

D Describe the differences in style between Friends of the Earth and Greenpeace (10.23).

E Discuss whether CND are jumping on the Chernobyl bandwagon.

10.20

Steam age ticket for a nuclear future

STEAM ENGINES and nuclear energy may not seem the most natural combination, but they were brought together this weekend, the first anniversary of the Chernobyl disaster.

British Nuclear Fuels laid on The Flying Scotsman, a brass band, and even a birthday cake to try to tempt people to make 'a journey from the past into the future.'

The nuclear industry admits that is has had an uphill struggle with its image since and perhaps before Chernobyl. So they used the popularity of steam trains in an attempt to ease anxieties about nuclear power . . .

Bob Phillipps, BNFL's senior Press officer, said: 'We have known for several years that we have had a problem of public attitude. We have decided to deal with things in an organised sophisticated way and yes, if you like, to popularise what we do.

'We want people to know they do not have to visit Sellafield in a radiation suit or with a geiger counter in their hands. If we reach 100,000 visitors that would put Sellafield very high on, say, the list of stately homes visits.'

Source: *The Independent*, 27.4.87

10.21

Train protest: Police stop a Greenpeace worker giving out leaflets on the Flying Scotsman bound for Sellafield's nuclear plant.

Source: *The Independent*, 27.4.87

10.22

Nuclear risks draw 50,000 to park rally

More than 50,000 people took part in the anti-nuclear rally in Hyde Park on Saturday to mark the first anniversary of the Chernobyl disaster.

The rally and the march to it from Victoria Embankment were organised by the Campaign for Nuclear Disarmament and Friends of the Earth coming together in their first mass rally.

At the start of the rally the crowd formed a symbolic anti-radiation symbol of triangles within a circle, crossed briefly by a red line of moving bodies . . . Two protestors scaled the Humber bridge yesterday and hung a banner saying 'Radiation Street' from its cables . . .

Three Greenpeace supporters were arrested after chaining themselves to the Flying Scotsman which was carrying 300 people to the Sellafield nuclear plant for a tour.

The CND in Wales yesterday announced a campaign to persuade people to withold payment of 20 per cent of their electricity bills – equivalent to the proportion of power generated by nuclear reactors.

Source: Susan Tirbutt, *The Guardian*, 27.4.87

10.23

Hyde Park rally

...while the joining forces of Friends of the Earth and CND on the first anniversary of Chernobyl to organise a very successful joint demonstration in Hyde Park was warmly welcomed, this important act of solidarity was not easy for either organisation. Friends of the Earth felt under a lot of pressure since CND had simply decided off its own bat, without consulting either Friends of the Earth or Greenpeace, to hold its annual demonstration on the anniversary of Chernobyl. This opened it up to accusations of naked opportunism on the grounds that the Chernobyl accident had little *direct* connection with the business of ridding the world of nuclear weapons. On the other hand, many CND activists felt equally uneasy about the dilution of their fundamental aims. And Greenpeace (the only organisation unequivocally committed to campaigning against both nuclear weapons and nuclear reactors) made it a great deal harder for both CND and Friends of the Earth by refusing to take part – on the tenuous and seemingly narrow-minded ground that 'demonstrations are not our style'.

Source: Jonathon Porrit and David Winner, *The Coming of the Greens*, Fontana, London, 1988 p. 18

10.24

Source: Critical Mess, *Links 26*, Third World First, Oxford, 1986

F. Conclusion

At the beginning of this unit I asked how the nuclear energy debate has affected British politics, and in turn how British political structures have affected the nuclear power issue.

One important effect on British politics has been to provide a focus for ecological activity out of which has sprung the Green movement.

Growing criticisms from ecologists and left wing fears about links with nuclear weapons put nuclear power on the ideological defensive, and failings in British reactor designs have hamstrung the once pace-setting industry. The industry has survived, although its formerly extensive plans for expansion have been largely halted.

The interest groups supporting nuclear power have been stronger than those groups campaigning in opposition. The Labour Party is divided on the issue while the Conservatives have seen political advantage in developing nuclear power.

Whatever else has happened, the nuclear industry has been forced to be much more open. It is ironic that these days the industry seeks to overcome the economic and political problems that it faces by trying to justify itself as a means of fighting the 'Greenhouse Effect'.

Further reading

Walter Patterson, *Nuclear Power*, (2nd edition), Penguin, Harmondsworth, Middlesex, 1987
Tony Hall, *Nuclear Politics*, Penguin, Harmondsworth, Middlesex, 1986
Gerald Foley, *The Energy Question*, (3rd edition), Penguin, Harmondsworth, Middlesex, 1987
Fred and Geoffrey Hoyle, *Commonsense in nuclear energy*, London, Heinemann, 1980
L. Mackay and M. Thompson (ed), *Something in the Wind-Politics after Chernobyl*, Pluto Press, London, 1988
Roger Williams, *The Nuclear Power Decisions*, Croom Helm, London, 1980